Living LANGUAGE

GRAMMAR

Michael Jago

Hodder & Stoughton

A MEMBER OF THE HODDER HEADLINE GROUP

Acknowledgements

The author, editors and publishers would like to thank the following:

Text 2: from *The Pickwick Papers* by Charles Dickens; Text 4: from *Ulysses* by James Joyce; Text 5: Skoda advert found in *The Radio Times* 27 June–3 July 1992; Text 6: from *1984* by George Orwell, Secker & Warburg Ltd, 1949; Text 7: from *The Grapes of Wrath* by John Steinbeck, William Heinemann Ltd, 1939; Text 8: from *Diaries 1915–1918* by Siegfried Sassoon, ed. R Hart-Davies, Faber & Faber, 1983; Text 9: Taken from *The Times*, 4 August 2000 © The Met. Office; Text 10: extract from the article 'The Frying Game' by Chris Sharrant in *News North-West*, 24 May 2000, Associated Newspapers Ltd; Text 11: from *Sons and Lovers* by D H Lawrence; Text 12: from *The Old Man and the Sea* by Ernest Hemingway, Jonathan Cape Ltd, 1952. Hemingway Foreign Rights Trust 1952; Text 13: from *The BFG* by Roald Dahl, Puffin Books, 1984; Text 14: from *Harry Potter and the Chamber of Secrets* by J K Rowling, Bloomsbury Children's Books, 1999; Text 16: from *Rent Act 1977*, reproduced under the terms of Crown Copyright Policy Guidance issued by HMSO; Text 17: from *Weather Watch* by Dick File, Fourth Estate Ltd © 1990 Guardian News Limited & R F File; Text 18: from *Emu oil information* Marburg, Australia; Text 19: *The Prampsy Grindler* by Vera Shutka; Text 20: from *A Clockwork Orange* by Anthony Burgess, William Heinmann Ltd, 1962; Text 21: from *A Lot to Learn* by R T Kurosaka; Text 22: from a visitor's guide to Tambourine Mountain in Queensland, Australia; Text 23: from *Sociology Themes and Perspectives* by Haralambos and Holborn; Text 24: Front cover of *The Eastern Eye*, 4 August 2000, Eastern Eye Publications Ltd; Text 25: reproduced in *Studies in Scarlet* by John West, Casdec Ltd, Durham, 1994; Text 26: from *Landslides and Avalanches* by Terry Jennings, Belitha Press Ltd, 1999; Text 27: from *Hot Touch* by Deborah Smith, Bantam, 1990; Text 28: from *The Inheritors* by William Golding, Faber & Faber Ltd; Commentary on Text 28/Activity 45 owes to the ideas and discussions in the final chapter of *Explorations in the Functions of Language* by M A K Halliday, Edward Arnold Ltd, 1973; Text 29: from *Numerology – Your Love and Relationship Guide* by Sonia Ducie, Elemant Books Ltd, 1999; Texts 30 & 31: from *The Parent's A to Z* by Penelope Leach, Allen Lane, 1983. Reproduced with kind permission of Penelope Leach; Text 32: page from the *Soldier's Service and Pay Book* issued during World War II by The Ministry of Defence; Text 33: from the *Traveller's First Aid Handbook* by Dr Peter Roylance & Dr Frank Preston, The Reader's Digest Association Ltd, 1983/1985; Text 34: from *Viking Age England* by Julian D Richards, Batsford, 1991; Text 36: from *Sophie's World* by Jostein Gaarder translated by Paulette Moller, Phoenix House, 1995; Text 37: 'Terror at Internet firm as worker shoots seven' by Annette Witheridge, taken from the *Daily Mail*, 27.12.00, © Daily Mail; Text 38: from *The Bell Jar* by Sylvia Plath, Faber & Faber, 1976; Text 39: from *Cages* by Abdulrazak Gurnah; Text 40: from *Alias Grace* by Margaret Atwood, Virago Press, 1997; Text 41: from 'Weddings and Honeymoons' holiday brochure, 1998, produced by Airtours Holidays Ltd trading as Tradewinds; Text 42: from *Titus Groan* by Mervyn Peake, Vintage, 1998; Text 43: 'Light Hotel' by Peter Redgrove in *The Weddings at Nether Powers and Other New Poems*, Routledge & Kegan Paul Ltd.

Every effort has been made to trace copyright holders of material reproduced in this book. Any rights not acknowledged here will be acknowledged in subsequent printings if notice is given to the publisher.

Order queries: please contact Bookpoint Ltd, 130 Milton Park, Abingdon, Oxon OX14 4SB.
Telephone: (44) 01235 827720, Fax: (44) 01235 400454. Lines are open from 9.00am–6.00pm, Monday to Saturday, with a 24 hour message answering service.
Email address: orders@bookpoint.co.uk

British Library Cataloguing in Publication Data
A catalogue entry for this title is available from The British Library

ISBN 0 340 78100 9

First published 2001
Impression number   10 9 8 7 6 5 4 3 2 1
Year   2005 2004 2003 2002 2001

Copyright © 2001 Michael Jago

Cover photo from The Ronald Grant Archive
Typeset by Fakenham Photosetting Limited, Fakenham, Norfolk
Printed in Great Britain for Hodder & Stoughton Educational, a division of Hodder Headline Plc, 338 Euston Road, London NW1 3BH by J. W. Arrowsmith Ltd, Bristol

Contents

Preface

This book has a number of interrelated aims. It aims to provide students with a basic grounding in the grammar of the English language. It assumes that this knowledge is of little use in itself, but has enormous potential for the understanding of any text, whether fiction or non-fiction. It therefore also aims to develop students' skills in applying this grammatical knowledge with consequent insights into the structure of these texts. In addition, at certain key stages, it encourages students to be suitably critical of their own writing skills. And finally it aims to demonstrate – and this is the central premise of the whole book – that a knowledge of grammar is actually essential to a fuller appreciation of meaning; that meaning is not conveyed merely through lexical choices but also through grammatical choices.

The book has been written specifically for students engaged in the study of English at Advanced Level (both AS and A2) regardless of the particular Awarding Body. Though it is clearly central to English Language, students engaged in a joint Language and Literature course would also benefit considerably, particularly as grammar is explained in relation to real texts rather than as an end in itself. It is also hoped that students following other courses of a similar nature will find some useful guidance and instruction here.

No previous knowledge of grammatical terminology is assumed. Instead, the book initially draws and relies upon the intuitive grammatical knowledge that native speakers are often surprised to discover they possess! Every grammatical term and concept is emboldened, explained and exemplified when first introduced, and is comprehensively indexed to avoid any need for a glossary. Each chapter contains a deliberate mixture of exposition with invented examples, balanced by regular examination of real texts. As part of its focus on the importance of meaning in grammar, this book assumes that only by exploring real texts can students come to realise the importance of grammatical knowledge. A comprehensive range of activities is provided, many of which have detailed commentaries that themselves form an integral part of the book's structure. In the interests of making available further texts for study, a short appendix with some suggestions for approach has been added. However, students should be encouraged to seek out their own texts on every possible occasion.

Inevitably, in a book of this size, a careful balance has to be struck between breadth and depth of coverage. A guiding principle in the selection of content has been the perceived need to explain and exemplify topics in such a way as to allow students to develop their knowledge and skills at a realistic pace. This has necessitated the omission of some interesting aspects of grammar, but their inclusion, even if possible, would have quite likely overburdened an already ambitious volume. The following pages provide more than enough coverage of the fundamentals to allow students to progress with confidence to more detailed treatments of grammar elsewhere should they wish to.

As to grammatical terminology, there exists currently a perplexing number of terms, partly a result of the many different descriptions of grammar published during the last fifty or so years. Several of these terms are either superfluous or else overlap in sometimes confusing ways. This book has necessarily adopted some terms in preference to others, though it generally justifies its choices and also informs students of common alternative names. However, students should be reassured that Examiners for Awarding Bodies are fully aware of this excess of terminology, and will judge a student's use of any term on the basis of accurate and relevant application rather than by personal choice from a range of possible alternatives.

So: welcome to the colourful world of grammar!

1 The Glamour of Grammar

In this first chapter you will:

- discover what grammar is really about
- begin to uncover the surprisingly large amount you already know
- examine the basic unit of grammar: the sentence
- rewrite texts and collect your own material for investigation.

Glamour?

You've probably never thought of grammar as remotely glamorous, but unlikely as it may seem, the words *grammar* and *glamour* are closely connected. In the past what was glamorous was magical. *Glamour* was a Scottish form of the word *grammar*, and anyone who knew or studied grammar was seen by the illiterate as magical, mysterious, even a little suspicious. Grammar still remains mysterious to many people, and this itself is a mystery because without grammar your ability to speak or write would be virtually non-existent. On the assumption that you *do* speak and write, and that you *can* understand both what people say and what people write (this book for example), then this means you must know quite a bit about grammar already, which is definitely good news!

So what exactly is grammar and what do you know about it? These are the first two questions that you are going to answer. A number of students were each asked to compose a sentence that they considered ungrammatical in some way. Here are just a few of their responses:

TEXT 1

1 He never got no chips.
2 Horse ran race won.
3 Giant three the the poisoned witches.
4 She done the dishes while we was watching the telly.
5 I want to buy her clothes.
6 Some giraffes love to race in hot-air balloons.
7 He's gotta go now.
8 The before is slowly.
9 That's between you and I.

ACTIVITY 1

1 Working in pairs, make a list of those sentences you think are ungrammatical. Then examine your list more closely and identify the particular feature in each sentence that you think makes it ungrammatical.
2 Compare your findings with another pair and reach agreement on any initial differences that you found.

3 In larger groups or as a class compare your responses. Which sentences caused most disagreement?

When you have completed this activity, read the commentary at the end of this chapter. Then read on.

Meaning versus structure?

This deceptively simple activity has allowed you to uncover some of the features that make a sentence grammatical. Some observations you may have made are:

1 Word order is vitally important.
2 Omission of some words doesn't necessarily prevent understanding.
3 Some word orders can't occur.
4 Different practices or conventions sometimes apply to speaking and writing: what is appropriate to one may not be appropriate to the other.

There clearly exists quite a close connection between meaning and structure. And it is this connection that forms the cornerstone of this book. Many textbooks maintain a strong distinction between the study of meaning in language (or **semantics**) and the study of structure in language (or **grammar**). They are both fundamental components of language and can certainly be studied separately, but in learning about grammar you will also come to appreciate how it is so often inseparable from meaning. In the meantime, we can conclude that sentences 2, 3 and 8 are fundamentally **un**grammatical.

ACTIVITY 2

1 On your own write a sentence that you believe has no meaning but is structurally sound, in other words grammatically perfect.
2 Present your example to a group or to the class, and be prepared to defend it.
3 In the light of your examples, discuss

whether or not you think it is possible to compose such a sentence.

Read the brief commentary on this activity at the end of the chapter. Then read on.

I didn't know I knew that!

Your discussions of these sentences will have shown that you clearly possess a knowledge of grammar that allows you to recognise whether or not a sequence of words is grammatical. You should not underestimate this discovery! Your unconscious ability to discriminate is the essential foundation for a conscious understanding of more intricate aspects of grammar. In fact, without a knowledge of grammar you wouldn't be able to speak or understand language. All that remains is for you to learn how to tap into this knowledge, so that you can then relate it to various grammatical terms, some of which you may have heard before (e.g. verb, conjunction, passive, interrogative) and some perhaps not (e.g. transitive, auxiliary, finite). Don't be put off by these words. All subjects need a set of precise technical terms to enable you to understand and discuss them. If, for instance, you are studying psychology you will need terms such as *behaviourism, complex, reinforcement, gestalt, imprinting,* and *operant conditioning;* if you are interested in computing then you will need *e-mail, megabyte, monitor, online, RAM,* and *software.* It's impossible to think about or discuss these or any other subjects efficiently without a specific technical vocabulary or **jargon**. The study of language, and of grammar in particular, is no exception.

As an example of this unconscious knowledge, let's take a closer look at just one aspect of grammar: the ways in which people describe how someone does something in the present rather than in the past or the future. First here's a brief note on the conventional way of presenting this information. **Linguists** (people who study language) refer to the particular someone as a **person**. So:

- First Person   I (singular); We (plural)
- Second Person   You (singular or plural, depending on context)
- Third Person   He, She, It (singular); They (plural).

Notice also that each person has what linguists call **number**, in other words there may be one person (singular) or more than one (plural). Applying this framework to the present tense of any verb describing an action, say for instance 'to laugh', gives:

	Singular	Plural
First	I laugh	We laugh
Second	You laugh	You laugh
Third	He/She/It laughs	They laugh.

Rather unremarkable, you might think. The verb is unvaried except in the third person singular which has the extra letter 's' at the end. You never have to check whether to add the 's'; you write it automatically and most of you will also pronounce the 's' automatically. By the same token you're unlikely to make slips by adding the 's' where it doesn't occur. Clearly there's a simple pattern here, and this pattern recurs again and again, regardless of the particular verb. So even though you may not have come across the term 'person' before, unconsciously you'll have known that this pattern, or rule, exists. But that's not the end of the story. In some parts of the UK (e.g. Berkshire), you'll hear local people add the 's' to *all* persons, both singular and plural. They will say 'I laughs', 'you laughs', and so on. Conversely, in other regions (e.g. Norfolk) you won't hear an 's' at all, even in the third person singular. In each case what you would be hearing (for almost invariably these forms occur today only in speech) would be a different regional pattern or rule. Such regional forms, called dialects, use slightly different rules. Their speakers automatically follow their own rule; they don't have the option to switch across to another. Only in writing do we nowadays all keep to the same rule, which is that the third person singular must add an 's' to the verb.

Right rules in right places

'But which is right?' you may be wondering. After all, we are so used to being told that our spelling is wrong, our pronunciation is wrong, and of course that our grammar is wrong. Well, the idea of telling tens of thousands of people in a particular region that the way they've been speaking all their lives is wrong seems rather foolish, not to say arrogant, and in any case would serve no useful purpose. As far as the spoken word is concerned there exist countless varieties of English around the world, each having its own set of rules. Each set regulates the way in which its speakers produce language, but there is no good reason to believe that any one set does a better or worse job than any other set. Ultimately, they all do the same job. So long as all speakers in a region agree to follow the same rules, there can be little danger of serious misunderstanding arising among them.

The situation is not the same when we consider written language. Here a (fairly) universally agreed form called **Standard English** has evolved. By and large this avoids variations such as the different present tense verb forms that we described earlier. Standard English certainly represents a distinct social advantage in that people from around the UK can communicate using a variety of written English that includes a standardised grammar and spelling. However, an unfortunate consequence has been the widespread downgrading in many people's eyes (or should we say, to many people's ears) of the other localised 'non-standard' varieties spoken around the UK. This downgrading in perception from non-standard to 'sub-standard' simply reflects social prejudice rather than any true understanding of how language actually works. Consider for example the widespread negative attitudes within the UK towards people who speak in a Birmingham or Liverpool dialect.

Language itself has been described as 'a rule-governed system'; in other words it is a system of using words in predictable patterns. But we have just seen (page 3) that it isn't only Standard English that obeys these rules; all varieties of English possess rules of one sort or another. The study of grammar is the study of these rules and patterns, and the ways in which they can affect meaning. Clearly all varieties, written or spoken, can be studied wherever they occur: an article in a national newspaper or a poem in the Devonshire dialect, the speech of a barrister in a courtroom or the conversation of a Yorkshire farmer. Each variety of English suits certain people for certain purposes – that's how each continues to exist.

Grammar: an examination . . .?

A grammar doesn't come as a free gift with a language – someone has to compile it! Such a task wasn't possible until writing was invented as a means of recording and preserving thought. How do linguists go about compiling a grammar? Essentially, in an objective and very systematic way. They record, describe and try to explain the recurring patterns that they detect in the language. Their purpose is said to be fundamentally **descriptive**. They describe the various grammatical constructions that people actually use, whether in the Cumbrian dialect or Standard English, but they're not concerned with how people *feel* about these grammatical constructions and they don't make value judgements about their relative worth or efficiency.

. . . or a remedy?

In stark contrast there exists another perspective, primarily associated with Standard English. Since the eighteenth century, several highly literate and respected people have at various times proposed a number of extra 'rules' in their attempt to improve the style and accuracy of other writers. Typical examples of constructions they have condemned are:

- the infamous 'split infinitive', e.g. 'to *quietly* laugh'. The recommended construction would be 'Quietly to laugh' or 'To laugh quietly'
- ending a sentence with a preposition, e.g. 'What did you write *with*?' The recommended construction would be 'With what did you write?'
- beginning a sentence with 'and' or 'but', e.g. '*But* she left'. A recommended alternative would be 'However, she left'.

These recommended 'rules' have nothing to do with how people actually use the language or how the language actually *works*. Rather they represent an attempt to impose artificial patterns upon the language in the belief that it somehow needs correction and improvement. Such 'rules' are termed **prescriptive** and represent the highly authoritarian view that people ought to use language in a particular way both now and in the future. Just as you are expected to obey the instructions about dosage and frequency on a doctor's prescription in order to improve your health, so you are expected to obey these 'rules' of language in order to improve your writing. Today many people see prescriptive 'rules' as largely misguided and irrelevant.

You'd probably agree that the educational system should provide the necessary instruction to enable everyone to write in a consistent and understandable manner, but many prescriptive 'rules' make no difference to the efficiency of communication and are at best purely stylistic. These very different viewpoints, the descriptive and the prescriptive, are still fiercely debated, but they needn't concern you further in this book. You simply need to remember that every non-standard form of English, with its individual patterns, has its own grammar. These various grammars will necessarily sometimes conflict with the grammar of Standard English, the form you'll have been taught to use in writing. This book is not intended to be prescriptive – though you may find many rules discussed that you will sometimes want to follow. It's far more concerned with exploring some of the grammatical variation that exists to influence intended meaning.

ACTIVITY 3

1 In small groups discuss what you now understand by the term grammar, and draft a working definition that takes account of everything relevant that you've read in this book so far. Allow at least 15 minutes for this task.

2 As a class compare your definitions and reach agreement on a final version.
3 Now turn back to Text 1. Which of the nine sentences represents merely the breaking of a prescriptive 'rule'?

Macro and micro

There's another important aspect of grammar that you will need to be aware of. So far we've talked about structure in terms of the way words are combined to form patterns. We've overlooked the separate words themselves as if they're unchanging. But of course this isn't true. In fact you've already looked at how the present tense of verbs can add or omit a final 's'. There are numerous ways in which individual words undergo changes of one sort or another. Fairly straightforward examples are the 's' added to most nouns to indicate plural (e.g. book → books) or the 'ed' added to most verbs to show that something occurred in the past (e.g. laugh → laughed). These aren't merely spelling variations like the choice between *lovable* and *loveable* or *jail* and *gaol*, where the different letters don't in any way change the meaning; they are clearly far more significant.

This idea of structure, then, can apply equally to individual words and to strings of words. Grammar is about the way you can build both words and sentences. As each of these aspects is very large in scope, linguists have given them different names: the study of word structure they call **morphology**; the study of how words are combined to form longer stretches of meaning they call **syntax**. In this book we shall be concentrating on syntax.

Joined-up thinking

So, grammar is about the different types of language patterning that speakers and writers choose. When you join up your thoughts to form a stretch of spoken or written language, you are constructing what linguists call a **text**. It's useful to remember that the words 'textile' and 'text' are closely related. Both are woven together, one with strands of various materials like wool, silk or cotton, the other with strings of words. The choice and meaning of individual words supply the separate colours in the text, but the particular grammatical combinations of these words produce the patterns that reflect the final unique composition. How do you begin to explore these patterns? Well, one way would be to examine individual words first, then move on to small groups or phrases, progress to longer groups or clauses, and so on. But that somewhat longwinded method doesn't allow for the intuitive knowledge that you are able to bring to this subject. So we'll begin by taking an overview of a larger structure, one with which you are already familiar: the **sentence**. The sentence is the key structure in grammar. Like other deceptively simple terms in language studies such as *syllable* and *word*, it's actually quite difficult to define easily and comprehensively, so we'll start from a traditional standpoint and then look at alternative ideas.

Some of you may recall from your earlier schooldays some such definition of the sentence as 'a group of words that expresses a complete meaning' or 'a set of words that stands alone and makes complete sense'. Sadly, these aren't too helpful. On the other hand, a sentence has also been defined as 'a set of words that begins with a capital letter and ends with a full stop'. Hardly better, is it? So instead, let's look at a couple of texts that include some questionable sentence structures. Text 2 is an extract from *The Pickwick Papers* by Charles Dickens, in which Mr Jingle impresses his listeners with his storytelling ability; Text 3 is an extract from an advertisement for a skin lotion for women.

TEXT 2

[1]'English girls not so fine as Spanish – noble creatures – jet hair – black eyes – lovely forms – sweet creatures – beautiful.'

[2]'You have been in Spain, sir?' said Mr. Tracy Tupman.

[3]'Lived there – ages.'

[4]'Many conquests, sir?' inquired Mr. Tupman.

[5]'Conquests! [6]Thousands. [7]Don Bolaro Fizzgig – Grandee – only daughter – Donna Christina – splendid creature – loved me to distraction – jealous father – high-souled daughter – handsome Englishman – Donna Christina in despair – prussic acid – stomach pump in my portmanteau – operation performed – old Bolaro in ecstasies – consent to our union – join hands and floods of tears – romantic story – very.'

[8]'Is the lady in England now, sir?' inquired Mr. Tupman, on whom the description of her charms had produced a powerful impression.

[9]'Dead, sir – dead,' said the stranger, applying to his right eye the brief remnant of a very old cambric handkerchief. [10]'Never recovered the stomach pump – undermined constitution – fell a victim.'

TEXT 3

[1]*In today's fast-paced world, our bodies face increasingly harsh challenges:
air pollution, central heating, air conditioning, artificial light
and solar radiation.*
[2]*Our sensitive skin becomes dehydrated and lifeless.*

[3]Dermaco responds with
MOISTURE SALVE REHYDRATION-EXTRA
An incredibly light, soft daytime lotion with

moisturising and remedial properties.

[4]*Soothes and protects skin from very first application.*

[5]*Concentrated with safe organic plant extracts*

and vitamins renowned for their therapeutic effects

and promotion of a healthy

youthful skin. [6]*Pleasant and easy to apply,*

perfect for any skin type and for all ages.

ACTIVITY 4

1 In pairs, examine the sentences (which have been numbered for ease of reference) in one or both texts. Make a list of those you think are definitely sentences and those which in some way seem doubtful.
2 Now look more closely at the doubtful list and identify what specifically has caused your doubts.

3 In groups compare your responses. You should reach agreement on your division of the sentences and discuss what you see as the essential difference between the two lists.

Read the commentary at the end of this chapter and then continue.

Cutting the sentence string in two

One of the observations made earlier in this chapter (page 2) was that the omission of some words doesn't necessarily prevent understanding (e.g. sentence 2 in Text 1). In other words, the fact that you can understand a group of words between a capital letter and full stop doesn't automatically make it acceptable *grammatically*. The assumption that comprehension and grammatical precision always go hand in hand is completely unfounded and represents a common stumbling block to identifying grammatically well-formed sentences.

Traditionally, in written English, a number of conditions must be fulfilled before you can call any string of words a sentence. In essence, a sentence mentions something and then says something else about that something. In its simplest form the something that's mentioned names or refers to a person, a place, an object or an idea (e.g. the judge, the courtroom, the wig, or justice). Technically it's called the **subject**. The something else that's said about it must include a **verb**, though in addition there are often other types of word that we'll examine in later chapters. The verb's job is to express an action (e.g. to slip, to yodel, to collapse, to catch), a process (e.g. to grow, to remember, to rule, to educate), or a state of existence (e.g. to seem, to belong, to exist, to be). Because it must include a verb, this second part is technically called the **verb phrase**. Put the two together and you have for example 'The judge yodelled', 'The courtroom collapsed', 'The wig slipped', or 'Justice rules'. You are then free to lengthen and elaborate these examples by adding further words (e.g. 'The judge yodelled in the bath' or 'The courtroom collapsed in a cloud of dust') but the basic two-part structure remains intact. This by no means exhausts the conditions for a sentence, but it will be enough for a re-examination of those sentences previously identified as doubtful in Texts 2 and 3.

Returning to Text 2 you can see that each of the doubtful sentences lacks one of the two necessary components. To take one example: sentence 3 contains no subject. Of course the reader knows that the speaker is referring to himself and so can mentally fill in the missing 'I'. The meaning is therefore perfectly clear from the context, but because the subject has not been explicitly mentioned, the sentence is *grammatically* incomplete. Similarly, sentence 10 does not refer to Donna Christina, only to what happened to her, but again the context makes the meaning immediately apparent. Another observation made earlier in this chapter was that different practices or conventions could apply to the spoken and the written word. Though Text 2 is written, it is clearly attempting to mimic some aspects of speech, even if they are of an eccentric nature. In addition, one-word sentences such as 5 and 6 are not uncommon in conversation.

You would probably consider it quite normal in speech to omit constant references to the same subject when everyone knows it is the topic of the discussion. In Text 3 it should now be plain that each of the three doubtful sentences (4–6) contains no mention of the subject, though much extra description is provided in order to sell the product concerned. Again the context makes it perfectly clear what is being referred to, and in fact it would appear heavy-handed, even ludicrous, if each sentence began with a repetition of such a lengthy product name. (Try it!) Frequently, and particularly in speech, we tend to leave out one or more words that we believe don't need to be mentioned or repeated in order to convey our meaning. This omission is known technically as **ellipsis**.

This first chapter has included a number of fundamental observations and ideas that are crucial to your understanding and your success in subsequent chapters. Don't be too surprised if you find you need to re-read some of it. You should certainly undertake some of the activities suggested on the next page before you move on to Chapter 2.

ACTIVITY 5

1 In small groups, make a list of types of text in which you would expect the sentences to be grammatically complete, incomplete, or a mixture of each. For example, you might expect a young child's picture book or storybook to contain only full, correct sentences, but classified advertisements in newspapers to contain a high proportion of incomplete sentences. Other texts to think about would include newspaper headlines, recipes, dictionary entries and e-mails.

2 Over a set time, say a week, collect as many different examples as you can of these types of text. Bring them in for a class discussion of the reasons for the grammatical differences.

ACTIVITY 6

1 On your own, rewrite Text 2 so that each sentence is grammatically complete. You will have to add a number of words, but you should as far as possible retain those already contained within it.

2 Is it possible to complete this task without increasing the number of sentences?

3 In small groups, compare and discuss your rewritten versions. What is lost from them and what is gained when you compare them with the original?

And finally, here are two texts for further practice. Text 4 is an extract from the novel *Ulysses* by James Joyce, in which a central character, Leopold Bloom, is thinking to himself as he walks through Dublin. Text 5 is an advertisement from the *Radio Times* for a Skoda car.

ACTIVITY 7

1 On your own or in pairs, choose one of the texts and identify all the sentences that are grammatically correct and all those that aren't.

2 In small groups, compare your lists and reach agreement. You should then discuss the reasons for the high proportion of ungrammatical sentences in the text. What has the writer set out to achieve by their choices of sentence structure?

TEXT 4

Houses, lines of houses, streets, miles of pavements, piledup bricks, stones. Changing hands. This owner, that. Landlord never dies they say. Other steps into his shoes when he gets his notice to quit. They buy the place up with gold and still they have all the gold. Swindle in it somewhere. Piled up in cities, worn away age after age. Pyramids in sand. Built on bread and onions. Slaves. Chinese wall. Babylon. Big stones left. Round towers. Rest rubble, sprawling suburbs, jerrybuilt, Kerwan's mushroom houses, built of breeze. Shelter for the night.

No one is anything.

This is the very worst hour of the day. Vitality. Dull, gloomy: hate this hour. Feel as if I had been eaten and spewed.

TEXT 5

A few of my Favorit things.

◉ FAMILY Sundays. A drive through the lush green of the Vale of Evesham. GAMES on the way. I-SPY with my little eye something beginning with F. Too easy. MISS a turn. How many white cars will we pass in the next two minutes? SPOTTING another Favorit. WAVES and smiles. SOMEBODY else who recognises 1.3 litres of value when they see it. TURNING in at the gate. HAPPINESS tinged with sadness at the journey's end. WISH they lived a bit further away. KISSES all round. THE children discover how much they've grown since Mum and Dad saw them last before they're swallowed by the garden. TEA and tittle-tattle in the conservatory. COOLING our feet in the stream. MOUTHWATERING aromas wafting down to us from the house. LUNCH. LAUGHTER. FRESH vegetables, picked by Dad that morning. WHY does her gravy taste so much better than mine? FAMILY discussions (never arguments). SUBJECTS range from potty-training to politics to the price of cars. NOBODY believes we paid so little for so much. BOB takes his brother for a spin. IMPRESSED, but still not convinced. HE always was a slow learner. HOMEWARD bound, five gears eating up the miles. SEE you all again soon. VERY soon. ◉

COMMENTARY
On Activity 1

One approach to this task is to distinguish between meaning and structure, in other words between whether the words as a group convey a meaning and whether they are organised into a recognisably possible pattern. A table may help make this clear.

Sentence	Meaning	Structure	Comments on key features
1	✔	✔	**never . . . no**: 'double' negative typical of spoken dialect
2	✔	✘	**The . . . the . . . and**: words missing, but the basic meaning is conveyed
3	✘	✘	Words in purely random order
4	✔	✔	**done . . . was**: typical of spoken dialect
5	✔	✔	Ambiguity: two meanings possible
6	✔	✔	Definitely strange, but perfectly understandable
7	✔	✔	**He's . . . gotta**: typical of colloquial speech
8	✘	✘	This word order isn't possible
9	✔	✔	Meaning and structure appear unremarkable.

It seems that the meaning and the structure of a sentence are often, though not always, closely interlinked. Sentences 2, 3 and 8 are each disorganised in their own way in terms of word order; the others require some separate comment before we can examine just what we mean by the term *grammatical.*

Sentences 1, 4, 7 and 9 are perfectly appropriate and commonplace in speaking, representing examples of regional dialect (1 and 4) or of everyday colloquial speech (7 and 9). However, they wouldn't be appropriate in writing of a more formal nature, though arguably this is no longer so true of sentence 9. The correct meaning of sentence 5 could only be discovered from the **context**. Context is an essential concept for understanding texts. It refers to the relevant knowledge that the writer or speaker assumes the reader or listener to possess. It also refers to the text currently being read by the reader or the conversation currently being engaged in jointly by the speaker and listener. And finally it includes the physical situation and the general circumstances in which reading or speaking occurs. So, if Sentence 5 were spoken, the shared background knowledge as well as the speaker's vocal intonation and stress would make the intended meaning clear; if it were written, the accompanying sentences would make it clear. Notice the crucial difference between this and sentence 3, in which the words need to be rearranged in order to convey either of two possible meanings ('The giant poisoned the three witches' or 'The three witches poisoned the giant'). Simply saying all the right words is not enough for successful communication; you must say them in the right order! Sentence 2 lacks some words but can still be understood as it stands, while sentence 8 (unlike sentence 3) cannot be rearranged in any sensible way. And though admittedly strange, sentence 6 could quite easily appear in a piece of surreal fiction.

COMMENTARY

On Activity 2

The American linguist Noam Chomsky suggested what he believed was an example of a meaningless but grammatically correct sentence: 'Colorless green ideas sleep furiously.' This now famous sentence contains contradictory meanings and yet seems to follow the natural word order of English. It has been the subject of endless debate, so if you're unsure whether it's grammatically correct, you are not alone! We'll return to this sentence later in this book (page 63).

COMMENTARY

On Activity 3

Sentence 9 in Text 1 breaks a prescriptive 'rule' involving pronouns. Prescriptivists would insist that people use the phrase 'between you and *me*'.

COMMENTARY

On Activity 4

You have probably divided the sentences in each text as follows:

	Grammatical	Doubtful
Text 2		
Sentence no.	2, 4, 8, 9,	1, 3, 5, 6, 7, 10.
Text 3		
Sentence no.	1, 2, 3,	4, 5, 6.

However, whether or not you finally agreed upon this split, you should have found some sentences problematic. Real texts, as opposed to texts invented purely to demonstrate grammatical rules, will usually contain something that doesn't quite 'fit', but this often proves more useful for real understanding. Of the doubtful sentences in Text 2, four (1, 3, 7 and 10) contain dashes to indicate the jerky and broken delivery of the speaker. But clearly there are considerable gaps in his story, reflected in the high number of missing words. The story has been reduced effectively to a 'note-form' account that is barely coherent; there is a narrative structure, but not a grammatical one. The remaining problematic sentences (5 and 6) are each of only one word, but if you've not identified these as doubtful, don't worry. We'll discuss them on page 9. In Text 3 you may have thought that there was an extra sentence between sentences 3 and 4 beginning 'An incredibly . . .'. However, you can see that advertisers use fonts and punctuation in unconventional – and sometimes misleading – ways, so you can't always rely on these features as a guide to the grammar. If you didn't identify the last three sentences as different in any sense to the first three, you now need to read pages 8–9 carefully.

Summary

In this chapter you have:

- discovered that you already possess an intuitive knowledge of grammar
- learnt some of the basic technical terms for the study of grammar
- examined the basic concept of the sentence in a range of texts.

2 From Small Beginnings . . .

In this chapter you will:

- learn a simple method for identifying two basic parts of a sentence
- begin to explore the variety of possible sentence structures
- uncover the fundamental sentence structure of English that you've always known
- analyse texts grammatically to discover their individual patterns.

Sentence sense

In Chapter 1 you saw something of the range of topics included in the study of grammar: syntax and morphology, prescriptive and descriptive grammar, standard and non-standard English, written and spoken language, and so on. This chapter concentrates on the grammar of texts written in Standard English, so that you first appreciate the basic principles before you go on to examine the ways in which writers and speakers can alter them for specific purposes. Let's first of all recap on a key point from the last chapter.

Our starting point is the two-part structure that we've identified as forming the basic sentence. The sentence contains a subject together with a verb phrase that says something about that subject. (Some other writers use the older term **predicate** for this second part, but we'll continue to use the term verb phrase.) Here's a simple example of such a sentence:

a   Tarquin guzzles ginger beer.

In such a short sentence you can probably sense without too much difficulty that the subject is 'Tarquin' and that what we learn about him, in other words the verb phrase, is that he 'guzzles ginger beer'.

Before we examine this sentence more closely, let's check that we can divide some further sentences into these two parts. The following short extract on the next page is from the novel *1984* by George Orwell; the sentences have been numbered for ease of reference.

TEXT 6

[1]The hallway smelt of boiled cabbage and old rag mats. [2]At one end of it a coloured poster, too large for indoor display, had been tacked to the wall. [3]It depicted simply an enormous face, more than a metre wide: the face of a man of about forty-five, with a heavy black moustache and ruggedly handsome features. [4]Winston made for the stairs. [5]It was no use trying the lift. [6]Even at the best of times it was seldom working, and at present the electric current was cut off during daylight hours. [7]It was part of the economy drive in preparation for Hate Week.

ACTIVITY 8

1 Individually or in pairs, divide each of the seven sentences into a subject and verb phrase. How does sentence 6 differ from the others?

2 In larger groups, compare your findings and agree your answers.

Read the commentary at the end of this chapter, and then continue.

Back to the booze!

This fairly straightforward two-part analysis is only the beginning. Let's return to our earlier sentence:

a   Tarquin guzzles ginger beer.

Now, instead of looking at the whole of the verb phrase, we're going to examine its most important component, the verb itself. The action taking place is conveyed by the verb, in this case 'guzzles', but of course other forms are possible (e.g. 'was guzzling', 'guzzled', 'will guzzle') to indicate other times when the action could occur (e.g. continuing in the past, completed in the past, in the future). **Tense** is the specific term used for this feature of time reference that verbs display. Unless the verb itself refers to the time when something happens, the sentence is grammatically incomplete. So for instance in

b   Tarquin guzzling ginger beer.

you cannot tell *when* the guzzling of the ginger beer takes place. You need some extra word or words inserted before 'guzzling' to clarify this, for example 'is', 'was', 'will be', or 'had been'. Again, remember that if you knew Tarquin or knew the context (i.e. the particular situation or set of circumstances) in which **b** was written or spoken, you would probably also know when the guzzling took place. But the point is that by itself **b** doesn't give you this information.

The verb must provide two more pieces of crucial information in order for the sentence to be grammatically complete. You've actually looked at these already on page 3, where you saw that the form of the verb could change depending on the person and the number. If you return to sentence **a** but omit Tarquin, you are left with

c   guzzles ginger beer.

You now don't know who the subject is, but the form of the verb does tell you three things. It tells you the time when this takes place (the present), it tells you the person (third) and it tells you the number (singular). All of this information is encoded in the single final 's' of 'guzzles'. If you were given the following options from which to choose a suitable subject for **c**, you would know that in Standard English only the last two could 'fit': *I, We, You, The thirsty prisoners, Tarquin, She*. A verb that provides this detailed information about the tense, person and number of a subject is called a **finite** verb. Actually, the word 'verb' can be misleading in that it implies that it's just one word, whereas we've seen that this isn't always the case. To overcome this possible source of confusion, linguists often use the term **verb group** instead, because the 'verb' is frequently composed of a small group of words (e.g. 'will be guzzling', 'has been guzzling', 'might have been guzzling').

English grammar – laughably easy!

It won't take you long to realise that the verb doesn't alter for every person and number. Actually it alters remarkably little. This doesn't change the fact that the verb indicates the three features mentioned; it just means that sometimes there would be greater uncertainty about the subject, *if the subject weren't mentioned*. So in

d   guzzle ginger beer.

you can't be sure of the person or number, except that it isn't third person singular. But of course this won't be a problem because the subject *will* be mentioned in a grammatically complete sentence, e.g.:

e   The thirsty prisoners guzzle ginger beer.

If at first this sounds complicated, it might be worth taking a look at how another language organises its finite verbs. The Roman soldiers who came to Britain two millennia ago spoke Latin. Here they are, laughing in the present tense:

	Singular	Plural
First person	rideo	ridemus
Second person	rides	ridetis
Third person	ridet	rident

The Latin grammatical system shows the distinctions between person and number far more clearly than the English (although in earlier times English itself was more complicated). Each person, singular and plural, is assigned an individual word ending. For example, the ending '-emus' tells you that 'we' are doing the laughing, not anyone else.

Before you look at a new text, let's check our understanding by examining just one sentence from Text 5 in Chapter 1:

f   Turning at the gate.

We want to know whether this is a complete grammatical sentence or not. We can readily identify 'Turning' as the verb describing the action, but is it finite? Hardly. By itself 'Turning' doesn't indicate tense, person or number. An expanded version could, for instance, read 'They were turning' or 'She will be turning'. And is there a subject? One simple method of finding the subject is to find the verb and ask: 'Who or what is turning?' The sentence doesn't tell us, so *grammatically* there is no subject. Of course, in the context of the advertisement we know that the implied subject is 'we' and that the implied tense is present. A grammatically complete version would therefore be 'We are turning at the gate'; however, we don't need that complete version for complete understanding of the meaning.

Now, if 'Turning' is a verb but isn't finite, you may be wondering what sort of verb it is. Unsurprisingly, it's called a **non-finite** verb. But what of the sentence we've just examined? If it's grammatically incomplete can we fairly call it a sentence at all? Well, conventionally it's simpler to call any string of words, enclosed by the customary punctuation of capital letter and full stop, a sentence. But to indicate that it lacks one or both of the elements that go to make up a full sentence, i.e. a subject and a finite verb, it's known as a **minor sentence**. (In contrast, a grammatically complete sentence is now sometimes referred to as a **major sentence**.) Minor sentences have always existed, but they have perhaps become increasingly common today within certain genres. They certainly occur frequently in speech. Apart from the minor sentence under discussion, did you notice another one in the previous paragraph? (Answer at end of chapter.)

Non-finite verbs occur very frequently in one of three forms:

- **Present participle**, invariably ending in '-ing' (e.g. *turning, laughing, crying, taking, writing, drinking, singing*).
- **Past participle**, usually ending in '-ed' (e.g. *turned, laughed, cried*), occasionally in '-en' (e.g. *taken, written*), and in a very small number of cases in an unpredictable form (e.g. *drunk, sung*).
- **Infinitive**, the basic form of the verb before any additions or alterations are made, often (but not always) preceded by the word 'to' (e.g. *turn, laugh, cry, take, write, drink, sing*). Remember Hamlet's '*To be* or not *to be*'?

Don't be misled by the words 'present' and 'past' in relation to the participles. These conventional descriptions are deceptive! As we've just discovered in examining sentence **f** above, the present participle 'Turning' *doesn't* indicate present tense. Another initial source of confusion that we must clear up is the difference between the simple past tense and the past participle, as they so often share the same form of the verb ending in '-ed'. Using the verb 'to turn' again, let's examine this difference in the two following sentences:

g   He turned the picture to the wall.
h   Turned to the wall, the picture . . .

Quite clearly, **g** indicates that the action of turning took place in the past. In contrast, **h** describes the picture as turned to the wall, but doesn't indicate when this action took place. We can show this by some of the possible ways of completing the sentence:

i   Turned to the wall, the picture had not been seen for centuries.
j   Turned to the wall, the picture now looks much improved.
k   Turned to the wall, the picture will be missed by no one tomorrow.

And so on. By themselves non-finite verbs *don't* indicate tense, person or number; they need help from other verbs. We'll be looking at exactly how this happens a little later (page 52).

Interim review

Let's just review and apply this method for identifying the key parts of a sentence. You'll need to feel confident in its application, as you will be developing it in later chapters. In its most basic form, the method is:

1 Find the finite verb.
2 Put 'Who or what?' in front of this finite verb to discover the subject.

These two simple stages should enable you to start dealing with most sentences. There will always be exceptions, but that's inevitable because language has virtually infinite possibilities. This method doesn't, for instance, apply to sentences that are commands (e.g. 'Take off that wig.'). Don't worry about them for now! So let's apply the method to two further sentences from Text 5. First:

l   Bob takes his brother for a spin.

Stage 1 The finite verb 'takes' expresses the action of the sentence.

Stage 2 Ask 'Who or what takes?' Answer 'Bob' = subject.

m   He always was a slow learner.

Stage 1 The finite verb 'was' expresses the state of existence.

Stage 2 Ask 'Who or what was?' Answer 'He' = subject.

You have identified the subject and the verb of each sentence, and have shown that each sentence is grammatically complete (and consequently not a minor sentence). Note, by the way, that we're not using the word 'subject' as a synonym for '**topic**'. In **l**, for example, the topic is 'a spin', because the whole text is about the virtues of driving the vehicle that's being advertised. The term 'subject' is a purely grammatical concept within the sentence. Very often the subject is also the topic, but this needn't be so. However, at this stage we don't need to examine this aspect further (see page 105).

'Tag, innit?'

Another useful way of checking that a sentence contains both a subject and a finite verb is to see whether you can add a **tag question** at the end. This will work only for statements (as opposed to questions or commands) but then statements do make up the vast majority of sentences. A tag question is quite simply a question, either positive or negative, which is tagged on or added to a statement, and which seems to question the fact just stated. For example:

n Bob takes his brother for a spin, *does he?* (or *doesn't he?*)

o He always was a slow learner, *was he?* (or *wasn't he?*)

You'll quickly realise that in each case you can add a tag question only if the sentence already contains both a subject and a finite verb. The tag question must incorporate the appropriate subject and tense. Faced with

f Turning at the gate.

it's plainly impossible to add a tag question as the relevant information is missing from this minor sentence.

Before you move on to explore more complicated types of sentence, here are some further texts for exploration. Text 7, which is an extract from John Steinbeck's novel *The Grapes of Wrath*, describes how a land turtle survives the murderous attempt of a sadistic truck driver. For your reference the sentences have again been numbered.

TEXT 7

[1]And now a light truck approached, and as it came near, the driver saw the turtle and swerved to hit it. [2]His front wheel struck the edge of the shell, flipped the turtle like a tiddly-wink, spun it like a coin, and rolled it off the highway. [3]The truck went back to its course along the right side. [4]Lying on its back, the turtle was tight in its shell for a long time. [5]But at last its legs waved in the air, reaching for something to pull it over. [6]Its front foot caught a piece of quartz and little by little the shell pulled over and flopped upright. [7]The wild oat head fell out and three of the spearhead seeds stuck in the ground. [8]And as the turtle crawled on down the embankment, its shell dragged dirt over the seeds. [9]The turtle entered a dust road and jerked itself along, drawing a wavy shallow trench in the dust with its shell. [10]The old humorous eyes looked ahead, and the horny beak opened a little. [11]His yellow toe-nails slipped a fraction in the dust.

ACTIVITY 9

1 In pairs, taking each sentence in turn, apply the two-stage method outlined on page 18 to identify all the subjects and finite verbs. Record your answers in a table for comparison later. Remember that a sentence may contain more than one of each. Is there always a one-to-one correspondence between subject and verb?

2 In pairs, re-examine each sentence and list any non-finite verbs present.

3 In small groups compare your tables and reach agreement. What variations in the patterning of subjects, finite verbs and non-finite verbs can you detect?

Read the commentary on this activity at the end of this chapter, then read on. Some further exercises for Text 7 are suggested in Activities 10 (3), 11 and 12.

Text 8 is from the diary of Siegfried Sassoon, a poet who fought during World War I. In this extract he records part of his journey from Ireland to Palestine in 1918. Text 9 is part of the weather information published in *The Times* on 4 August 2000. Text 10 is the opening of an article about food entitled 'The frying game' that appeared in the free newspaper *News North-West* on 24 May 2000.

TEXT 8

February 14 (On the train. Notes)

6.30 p.m. after reading Pater's 'Leonardo'. Train stops. Black smoke drifting. Got out for a minute. Trees against pale sky – clouds higher, with three stars. The others playing cards by candlelight. Scraps of talk – 'Twist – Stick etc' 'Any more for any more' (men drawing rations). Jock officer going back to Seventh Division. Halt at Bourges – French and English soldiers on platform. American camps on the way. Black men in khaki at Cherbourg. Brown landscapes.

The beginning of a new adventure. I am already half way into my campaigning dream life. Funny mixture of reality and crude circumstance with inner 'flame-like' spiritual experience. But this time I know myself, and am quite free to study the others – equipped to interpret this strangest of all my adventures – ready to create brilliant pictures of sunlight and shadow. In the 'awful brevity' of human life I seek truth.

TEXT 9

The weather today

General situation: Rather cloudy but most places fair, just a little rain or drizzle for a time in the north of Scotland and in some western coastal areas especially later. Bright or sunny spells developing.

Central Highlands, Argyll, NW Scotland, N Ireland: Rather cloudy with patchy rain early and later but also sunny spells developing. Wind southwest moderate. Max 22C (72F).

London, SE, Central S, Central N, E England, E Anglia, Midlands, Channel Islands: Mainly fair with bright or sunny spells. Wind northwest light or moderate. Max 22C (72F).

NE Scotland, Orkney, Shetland: Patchy rain and drizzle clearing away but returning late evening. Wind west fresh. Max 15C (59F).

SW, NW, NE England, Wales, Lake District, Isle of Man, Borders, Edinburgh and Dundee Area, SW Scotland, Glasgow, Moray Firth Area: Rather cloudy, but mainly dry. Bright or sunny spells developing. Wind west moderate. Max 21C (70F).

Republic of Ireland: Mainly fine with sunny spells but more cloudy early and late with a little patchy drizzle. Wind northwest fresh. Max 23C (73F).

Outlook: Mainly fair though rather cloudy. A little rain at times mainly in the north. Very warm where the sun breaks through.

TEXT 10

the frying game

FOOD AND DRINK

fish, chips and mushy peas to take away

Sometimes, nothing else will do. Not fancy modern British cooking, not authentic Thai cuisine, not rustic Italian with a touch of the River Café about it. Nothing, in fact, but that simplest of combinations – fish, chips and mushy peas. To take away, of course.

What makes the perfect fish supper? The cod should be fresh, white and flaky, the batter crisp to the bite and not too greasy; the chips crisp on the outside and fluffy on the inside; the peas mushy and moist, acting as part sauce, part vegetable. Add salt and malt vinegar and eat immediately – hanging about is a no-no.

There's no shortage of places in city centre Manchester to sample this British culinary institution. The quality, however, is anything but consistent.

ACTIVITY 10

1 In pairs, choose at least two of the three texts and identify all the major (i.e. grammatically complete) sentences and all the minor sentences. As a check on your accuracy, take each of the sentences you think is complete and add a tag question (but remember this won't work for questions or commands).

2 In small groups, compare your analysis and reach agreement. Taking each text in turn, examine the minor sentences and identify the parts that are missing (e.g. no subject, no finite verb, no verb at all). Discuss why you think the different types of ellipsis (see page 9) occur in each text. Do the texts vary in the amount of information that they leave unstated?

3 If you have earlier attempted Activity 9, you should now discuss how the types of ellipsis that you have just identified above differ from the types that occur in Text 7. Suggest reasons for any differences you detect.

4 As a group or class, brainstorm as many different types of personal writing in which you use some form of ellipsis. Discuss how the ellipsis differs (e.g. omission of subject or finite verb, reliance on information contained elsewhere in the text, reliance on the reader's knowledge) and why you use ellipsis. You might for instance consider how and why a note to the milkman differs from a lesson note made in class.

5 Individually, as a mini-project, collect examples of weather bulletins from a number of sources, both print (local and national papers) and electronic (teletext and website). Do all these texts follow the same pattern as Text 9? If not, why not? Prepare and give a five-minute presentation on your findings to your group or class.

What's the object?

Now that you've classified the sentence into some of its main components, you're ready to examine other parts in a little more detail. This in turn will allow you to become more aware of the types of pattern available to writers of different genres. At the moment we're still in the process of identifying larger rather than smaller components of the sentence. Let's return to Tarquin:

a   Tarquin guzzles ginger beer.

Already you are capable of discussing this sentence in grammatically meaningful ways. You can

- divide it into its subject 'Tarquin' and its verb phrase 'guzzles ginger beer'
- identify the verb group, in this case the single word 'guzzles'
- from the verb 'guzzles', identify its tense, person and number
- accordingly prove that the sentence is grammatically complete, and consequently not a minor sentence.

What's left to say? Well, what part does 'ginger beer' play in the sentence? Grammatically it's not absolutely essential because the sentence

p   Tarquin guzzles.

fulfils all the conditions of a complete sentence. We can see that 'ginger beer' extends the verb phrase, but it isn't a part of the verb. It identifies the object affected by the action of the verb, telling us in this case what exactly Tarquin guzzles. This component, which names or refers to the person, the place, the object or the idea that is directly affected by the action of the verb, is called the **direct object** (or simply **object** for short). To locate the direct object in any sentence, you simply take the verb and add 'Who or what?' So in **a**: 'guzzles who or what?' Answer: 'ginger beer'.

ACTIVITY 11

1 Look again at Text 7 on page 19. In pairs, but *omitting* sentences 4 and 5, list each verb in turn and locate any direct object. Don't expect every verb to be followed by one!

2 In small groups, compare your lists and reach agreement. What variations occur in the relationship of verb to direct object?

3 Before you read the commentary, identify any components about which you could not reach agreement, together with the reasons.

Now read the commentary at the end of the chapter, before reading on.

Howzat?

Text 7 has provided much useful information about sentence structure, but it still includes several chunks of text that don't seem to fit any of the components so far identified, i.e. subject, verb group or direct object. Let's now fill in the gaps and complete the jigsaw. First we need to revisit Tarquin. In the verb phrase of our basic sentence

a   Tarquin guzzles ginger beer.

we learn two things about the subject Tarquin: the activity he indulges in ('guzzles') and the object of his desire ('ginger beer'). However, the verb phrase could easily be further extended to provide even more information, should we so wish. It could tell us *when* he guzzles (e.g. 'today', 'soon', 'at night', 'on the Twelfth Day of Christmas'), *where* he guzzles (e.g. 'outdoors', 'here', 'behind the bushes', 'in the potting shed') or *how* he guzzles (e.g. 'with great delight', 'nervously', 'secretly', 'from a crystal glass'). Or of course it could tell us all three:

q   Tarquin guzzles ginger beer at night behind the bushes with great delight.

These three groups of words are therefore linked to the verb very closely, but they don't answer the question 'guzzles who or what?', they answer the questions 'guzzles *when*?' (about time), 'guzzles *where*?' (about place) and 'guzzles *how*?' (about manner). The answers to such questions are said to 'modify' the verb, in other words they add specific information about the verb. They are called **adverbials**, and can in fact answer a range of other questions, e.g. 'guzzles *why*?' ('because he feels thirsty', 'to satisfy his greed'), 'guzzles *how frequently*?' ('often', 'every Saturday afternoon'), or 'guzzles *with what result*?' ('to cure his indigestion'). However, adverbials of time, place and manner are particularly common. Notice finally how the above examples vary considerably in the number of words they contain, and that some also include their own verb, either finite ('feels') or non-finite ('to satisfy', 'to cure'). So let's now return to Text 7 and put this knowledge into practice.

ACTIVITY 12

1 In pairs re-examine Text 7 on page 19. (You'll find it helpful to have to hand your notes from Activity 11.) Again *omitting* sentences 4 and 5, take each verb as identified in the previous Activity and locate and list any adverbials by asking the relevant questions: When? Where? How? Why? etc. As with direct objects, you shouldn't necessarily expect to match one adverbial to each verb.

2 In small or large groups compare your results and discuss any differences. What preliminary observations can you make about the occurrence of adverbials?

3 If you delete all the subjects, verb groups, direct objects and adverbials from the nine sentences you have analysed, what repeated word remains? And what function does it have?

Turn to the commentary at the end of this chapter, and then read on.

Final review

Your progress through this chapter represents a considerable achievement. You are now able to analyse a stretch of writing into four fundamental parts that can be varied to produce a range of patterns. For simplicity, these four parts are conventionally referred to by capital letters: Subject (**S**), Verb (**V**), Object (**O**) and Adverbial (**A**). Here is a short sentence of just six words, which has been analysed to reveal these four components:

S   V   O   A

r   The dog / bites / the postmen / savagely.

1 In pairs, without altering the separate words at all, rewrite the above complete sentence by changing the order of the four parts in as many different ways as you can. Including **r**, there are in fact 24 different ways of reorganising them!

2 Using your intuition, classify the 24 sentences as either grammatically 'acceptable' (in other words grammatically correct and well-formed) or 'unacceptable'. You'll probably find you also need a 'doubtful' category for one or two versions that you'll be unsure about. Remember that the *meaning* of the original sentence must remain the same; it's always the dog that's doing the biting!

3 In larger groups or as a class review the degree of consensus on the 'acceptable' versions. Can you detect in these any regular pattern among the components?

4 Next examine any versions classified as 'doubtful' and discuss their essential difference from the 'acceptable' versions. How would you now describe the basic structure of a typical sentence in English?

When you have completed this Activity, read the commentary at the end of this chapter, then read on.

Exceptions no object!

For the sake of completeness we need to consider a relatively small number of exceptions to our earlier description of the direct object. We noted in Chapter 1 (page 4) that language is sometimes described as a 'rule-governed system', though this is arguably a somewhat idealistic view. Its rules often contradict logic and don't account for unexpected exceptions. There is, for example, a small group of verbs which certainly behave like other verbs in that a 'who' or 'what' can follow them. However, the 'who' or 'what' isn't called a direct object but a **complement**. Let's make it quite clear here that this doesn't upset what you've just learnt about the SVO structure of English. In fact some linguists actually lump direct objects and complements together under the one umbrella term of complement; that this book doesn't reflects the fact that the distinction is still commonly made, and also that it can prove quite useful as we'll see.

So when is a direct object not a direct object but a complement? Answer:

■ either when it shares the identity of the subject or another direct object
■ or when it describes some attribute of the subject or of another direct object.

Let's take this bit by bit. First of all, a complement adds further information about a subject or direct object already mentioned within the same sentence. Where a subject is involved, the finite verb serves to link or yoke the subject with its complement. It's called a **copular** (i.e. 'joining') **verb**, and some of the commonest are: *to appear, to be, to become, to feel, to look, to remain, to seem, to sound, to smell*. A few examples should make this clear:

s	Romulus *is* a glutton.
t	Romulus *was* excessively fat.
u	Romulus *sounds* breathless.
v	Romulus *seems* exceptionally greedy.

In all the above sentences what follows the italicised copular verb refers back to Romulus, either by identifying him in **s** or by describing him in **t** to **v**. But note that sometimes one of these verbs may also behave in the more usual way and be followed by a direct object. For instance, in

w	Romulus sounds the gong.

'the gong' is clearly not the same thing as the subject 'Romulus'. It neither identifies nor describes the subject and is therefore in this case a direct object. Conventionally, the symbol for a complement is **C**; the sentences **s** to **v** would therefore be analysed as SVC, whereas **w** would be SVO. Sometimes, however, a complement may refer to a direct object within the sentence. For example:

x	People call Romulus a glutton.
y	They called him greedy.

In these sentences the direct objects 'Romulus' and 'him' are immediately followed by a further description that refers to each of them, 'a glutton' and 'greedy', not to the subjects. Both sentences would therefore be analysed as SVOC. Note that the complement only *adds* information; it can't replace the direct object. For example, if we omit the direct object 'Romulus' from **x**, then

z	People call a glutton.

clearly doesn't convey the intended meaning.

Extra time

The following texts provide you with opportunities to make use of the grammatical knowledge you've so far tapped into. In the interests of realism each text is printed without omissions, so inevitably you'll occasionally find a group of words that you'll be unsure of (in all likelihood because they represent a pattern we've not yet examined). You shouldn't let this deter you. At this stage the important thing is to concentrate on the large sections that you *can* do, not on the small ones that you can't. Text 11 is an extract from *Sons and Lovers* by D H Lawrence, and introduces the reader to Baxter Dawes, husband of the woman with whom another character, Paul Morel, is to have an affair. Text 12 is from *The Old Man and the Sea* by Ernest Hemingway, and records part of the old man's struggle to survive while fishing at sea alone. Sentences have been numbered for your reference.

TEXT 11

[1]Baxter Dawes he knew and disliked. [2]The smith was a man of thirty-one or thirty-two. [3]He came occasionally through Paul's corner – a big, well-set man, also striking to look at, and handsome. [4]There was a peculiar

similarity between himself and his wife. [5]He had the same white skin, with a clear, golden tinge. [6]His hair was of soft brown, his moustache was golden. [7]And he had a similar defiance in his bearing and manner. [8]But then came the difference. [9]His eyes, dark brown and quick-shifting, were dissolute. [10]They protruded very slightly, and his eyelids hung over them in a way that was half hate. [11]His mouth, too, was sensual. [12]His whole manner was of cowed defiance, as if he were ready to knock anybody down who disapproved of him – perhaps because he really disapproved of himself.

TEXT 12

[1]Back in the stern he turned so that his left hand held the strain of the line across his shoulders and drew his knife from its sheath with his right hand. [2]The stars were bright now and he saw the dolphin clearly and he pushed the blade of his knife into his head and drew him out from under the stern. [3]He put one of his feet on the fish and slit him quickly from the vent up to the tip of his lower jaw. [4]Then he put his knife down and gutted him with his right hand, scooping him clean and pulling the gills clear. [5]He felt the maw heavy and slippery in his hands and he slit it open. [6]There were two flying fish inside. [7]They were fresh and hard and he laid them side by side and dropped the guts and the gills over the stern.

ACTIVITY 14

1 Individually, in advance of a lesson, prepare an analysis of both texts by subdividing each sentence into the five components you are now familiar with: S, V, O, A and C.
2 In small groups, compare your analyses and agree as far as possible on a final version. Make a note of any doubtful groups of words for subsequent reference.
3 Next make a list of as many grammatical similarities and differences between the two texts as you can, including the patterns displayed by their five components.
4 One member of each group should present the findings to the class, after which you should discuss the reasons for them and their significance.

To help you with this Activity, you'll find some clues (rather than a commentary) at the end of this chapter.

ACTIVITY 15

1 Individually, choose an extended piece of writing that you've completed during the last six months (fiction or non-fiction) and analyse a representative amount for its sentence structure.
2 What is the most common pattern that you use? Make a record of it, then do the same exercise with a similar piece that you wrote two years ago and compare the results. Do you detect any significant changes?
3 Keep this record and analyse a further piece of your writing in six months. Do you expect to find any changes? Do you *want* to make any changes?

COMMENTARY

On Activity 8

You should have found this a relatively straightforward activity, apart from sentence 6. The subjects of the seven sentences are:

1 The hallway
2 a coloured poster, too large for indoor display
3 It
4 Winston
5 It
6 it *and* the electric current
7 It

Everything else in each sentence makes up a verb phrase. Points to note at this stage are:

- although most sentences contain only one subject, it's possible for a sentence to include more than one (i.e. sentence 6)
- where there is just one subject, it occurs at or near the beginning of the sentence.

You should, however, be prepared for more complicated sentences that don't display these patterns.

COMMENTARY

On Activity 9

You should have been able to analyse the subjects and finite verbs in each sentence as follows:

Sentence	Subject	Finite verb
1	a light truck	approached
	it	came
	the driver	saw; swerved
2	His front wheel	struck; flipped; spun; rolled
3	The truck	went
4	the turtle	was
5	its legs	waved
6	Its front foot	caught
	the shell	pulled; flopped
7	The wild oat head	fell
	three of the spearhead seeds	stuck
8	the turtle	crawled
	its shell	dragged
9	The turtle	entered; jerked
10	The old humorous eyes	looked
	the horny beak	opened
11	His yellow toe-nails	slipped

Your analysis of non-finite verbs should have revealed the following:

Sentence	Non-finite verb
1	to hit (infinitive)
4	Lying (present participle)
5	reaching (present participle); to pull (infinitive)
9	drawing (present participle)

Some of the observations you might have made are:

- in general, considerable variety exists among the eleven sentences in the combinations of subject and finite verb
- among the sentences with only one subject, four are fairly straightforward in having just one corresponding finite verb (sentences 3, 4, 5 and 11), but two have additional finite verbs (sentences 2 and 9)
- three sentences contain two subjects, each with a corresponding finite verb (sentences 7, 8 and 10)
- more complicated patterns of subject and finite verb occur in sentences 1 and 6
- complete grammatical sentences can also include non-finite verbs separated from the finite verbs (i.e. as different verb groups: sentences 4, 5 and 9).

You should also have examined the sequence of subjects in terms of what they refer to, how many are repeated, and how these choices help create the description of the incident.

COMMENTARY
On Activity 11

You should have identified the following direct objects:

Sentence	Verb	Direct object
1	approached	*none*
	came	*none*
	saw	the turtle
	swerved	*none*
	to hit	it
2	struck	the edge
	flipped	the turtle
	spun	it
	rolled	it
3	went	*none*
6	caught	a piece of quartz
	pulled	*none*
	flopped	*none*
7	fell	*none*
	stuck	*none*
8	crawled	*none*
	dragged	dirt
9	entered	a dust road
	jerked	itself
	drawing	a wavy shallow trench
10	looked	*none*
	opened	*none*
11	slipped	*none*

The large number of verbs without a direct object may have surprised you. Alternatively, you may have identified direct objects where there are none; if so, check carefully your method for ascertaining the direct object. The 'who or what' must identify a person, a place, an object or an idea. You should also have noted that a non-finite verb can have its own direct object ('to hit' in sentence 1; 'drawing' in sentence 9).

COMMENTARY
On Activity 12

The adverbials you should have listed are:

Sentence	Verb	Adverbial
1	approached	now
	came	near
	saw	*none*
	swerved	to hit it
	to hit	*none*
2	struck	*none*
	flipped	like a tiddly-wink
	spun	like a coin
	rolled	off the highway
3	went	back to its course along the right side
6	caught	*none*
	pulled	little by little; over
	flopped	upright
7	fell	out
	stuck	in the ground
8	crawled	on down the embankment
	dragged	over the seeds
9	entered	*none*
	jerked	along
	drawing	in the dust with its shell
10	looked	ahead
	opened	a little
11	slipped	a fraction in the dust

Your initial observations should have included the following:

■ an adverbial can consist of just one word or a group of words
■ a verb can be modified by more than one adverbial
■ a verb may or may not have both a direct object and an adverbial.

You might also have made some comment on the particular frequency of adverbials relating to place and manner, as well as the positions they occupy relative to other components in the sentence. As for the word that remains after deletion of the various components, you should have found that 'and' occurs nine times, serving to link either parts of a sentence or consecutive whole sentences.

COMMENTARY
On Activity 13

This task was not especially easy and so should have provoked some initial disagreement about a small number of versions. You should certainly have agreed upon the following versions as 'acceptable': SVOA, SAVO, and ASVO. You may have classified the following as 'doubtful': SVAO, OASV, (and maybe one or two more), or you may have agreed to place one or two of these into the 'acceptable' list, but also marked them as highly unusual. However, you'll fairly quickly have discarded the vast majority of combinations as being 'unacceptable' in that they are both ungrammatical and poorly formed for conveying meaning easily. Understandable some of them may be, but as we discovered in Chapter 1 (page 8), the fact that we can understand a sentence doesn't by itself make that sentence grammatical.

Your discussion of sentence patterns should have allowed you to discover that the usual basic sentence structure in English can be represented by the sequence **SVO**, and that **A** can be inserted in a number of positions without affecting this order. Of course, some other combinations can occur, but they will have struck you intuitively as uncommon, to be used only in unusual circumstances for emphasis or special effect. They don't represent the norm. The English language shares this SVO structure with a large number of the world's languages, but not all. Many prefer a basic SOV sequence (e.g. Japanese and Latin), others a VSO sequence (e.g. Irish and Welsh).

How useful is this knowledge about the basic sentence structure of English? Well, once you've established the basic pattern, you will become more aware of deviations from it in a writer's work. Such deviations are clearly worth investigating in order to discover why the usual pattern has been avoided. They also provide one of the clues to the 'stylistic fingerprints' of a writer, the set of patterns and techniques that make a writer's work in some way unique. Apart from any basic deviations, another clue to individual style is the degree of complexity in the patterning of the four components within each sentence.

Clues for Activity 14

Some of the features you should examine are:

- number of words and sentences, as well as sentence length
- frequency of sentences with basic SVO or SVC structure (ignoring As)
- type and frequency of component in sentences (e.g. O v C)
- any sentences with unusual structure
- changes of subject within and between sentences.

There are others, but these five alone will provide plenty of scope for a revealing discussion on how the style of the two writers differs.

NOTE: The minor sentence in the paragraph on page 17 is 'Hardly.'

Summary

In this chapter you have:

- developed a system for analysing basic sentence structure
- analysed texts to discover some specific stylistic characteristics
- examined your own writing style over time.

3 ... Grow Giant Things

In this chapter you will:

- explore how sentence parts are variously interrelated
- discover some specific characteristics of legal writing
- apply your analytical skills to informative and promotional texts
- investigate the four types of sentence
- find your own texts for analysis.

TEXT 13

¹Sophie couldn't sleep.

²A brilliant moonbeam was slanting through a gap in the curtains. ³It was shining right on to her pillow.

⁴The other children in the dormitory had been asleep for hours.

⁵Sophie closed her eyes and lay quite still. ⁶She tried very hard to doze off.

⁷It was no good. ⁸The moonbeam was like a silver blade slicing through the room on to her face.

⁹The house was absolutely silent. ¹⁰No voices came up from downstairs. ¹¹There were no footsteps on the floor above either.

¹²The window behind the curtain was wide open, but nobody was walking on the pavement outside. ¹³No cars went by on the street. ¹⁴Not the tiniest sound could be heard anywhere. ¹⁵Sophie had never known such a silence.

Simplicity itself

You may well recognise the above text as the opening of Roald Dahl's *The BFG*. It makes few demands, you'd say, on the intended young readership, and if you were asked how this is achieved you might reply that the sentences are very simple. Well, most of the sentences *are* simple, but in a rather specialised sense. A sentence may be short, easy to understand, and contain only basic vocabulary, but these things in themselves don't make a simple sentence. Grammatically, a **simple sentence** is a complete sentence that contains a finite verb within its only verb group (see page 16). This means that of the fifteen sentences in the text, only twelve are simple in this grammatical sense.

1 In pairs, identify the verb groups in all 15 sentences of Text 13.

2 Next identify the 12 simple sentences and agree why the remaining three sentences aren't simple.

Check your answer with the commentary at the end of the chapter before reading on.

Simple sentences do tend to be fairly short, because it's difficult to lengthen them very much without introducing another verb. And this is where we really begin to recognise the variety of patterning possible within the sentence. One method of lengthening a sentence is to join two previously separate sentences. Sentence 12 in *The BFG* exemplifies this. You can see that there were actually two sentences:

a The window behind the curtain was wide open.
b Nobody was walking on the pavement outside.

They've been redrafted as one sentence, by inserting a comma together with the extra linking word 'but'. Of course, you can't join just any two sentences; some connection in meaning must already exist between them. The various elements of meaning within any sentence are quite closely related; that's why they're combined in one sentence. If you examine the combined version of **a** and **b** you'll see that it contains two finite verbs: 'was' and 'was walking' (its full structure is SVC + SVAA). The two simple sentences have become a **multiple sentence**, but so that you can still refer to the two parts, each previously separate sentence is called a **clause**. A moment's thought will tell you that a simple sentence is therefore *also* a clause, though it isn't normally referred to as such. Any sentence that contains a finite verb and at least one other verb (finite or non-finite) within a separate verb group is called a multiple sentence, so as to distinguish it from a simple sentence. However, as several kinds of multiple sentence exist, this basic distinction needs further refinement if it's to be of much use in analysis.

Let's return to our combined sentence 12 from the text. This particular kind of multiple sentence is called a **compound sentence**, and theoretically you could continue to add more related simple sentences, e.g. 'and no cars went by on the street'. The compound sentence is made up of two or more separate clauses, each of which contains a finite verb and is independent of the other clauses. In other words, each makes complete sense by itself whether or not it's joined to another clause, and each is of roughly equal importance in the whole sentence. Words used to link each clause are called **coordinators** though, as with many other grammatical terms, you may come across alternative names such as conjunctions and connectives. We discuss these further in Chapter 4 (page 56). The most common coordinators are 'and', 'or', 'but' and 'yet', together with the pairs 'either ... or' and 'neither ... nor'.

But compound sentences are more varied than you might at first imagine.

Look at sentence 5 from *The BFG*. This time the two sentences that have been linked must have been:

c   Sophie closed her eyes.
d   Sophie lay quite still.

The simplest connection of the two would be

e   Sophie closed her eyes and Sophie lay quite still.

but this sounds clumsy and unnecessarily repetitive to our ears (and isn't much improved by substituting 'she' for the second 'Sophie'). As both finite verbs share the same subject, its second mention has been dropped. Such ellipsis (see page 9) is normal and shouldn't disguise the fact that the sentence is compound in structure. Naturally, where the subjects are different, as in sentence 12 ('The window' and 'nobody'), ellipsis isn't possible. To summarise, we can say that a compound sentence consists of two or more **independent clauses**, each containing a finite verb. If we give an upper case (i.e. capital) letter to each independent clause, we could represent it as:

A + **B** + **C** + etc.

ACTIVITY 17

1   In pairs, rewrite Text 13 by combining all the simple sentences into a number of compound sentences. You should also consider altering and redrafting the two existing compound sentences. What is the smallest number of sentences possible that still allows the passage to sound natural?

2   In small groups, compare your versions and discuss the limitations on combining simple and compound sentences in this manner. Why has Dahl used so many sentences? In what ways do they vary and why?

Complex? It depends.

Believe it or not, you're now not far from understanding the basic framework or template for the construction of *all* sentences in English. Essentially, we just need to examine one more kind of multiple sentence called the **complex sentence**. Like the term 'simple sentence', this is a specific grammatical term, and is not an alternative phrase for 'complicated sentence' or 'long sentence'. Let's briefly revisit Tarquin:

f   *When he found some large bushes,* Tarquin drank his ginger beer.

If we examine this sentence, we certainly have two clauses, each with a finite verb. We'll also recognise that the first clause is functioning as an adverbial of time (page 23) to state when Tarquin did his drinking. But the crucial difference is that only the second clause is independent. The first cannot stand alone and make complete sense, even though it contains both a subject 'he' and a finite verb 'found'.

g   When he found some large bushes.

See! This first clause clearly needs an independent clause to explain what happened after he found the bushes, and predictably enough this first clause is called a **dependent clause**, because it depends on or needs another clause. Another method of lengthening a sentence, then, is to add further dependent clauses, none of which can stand on its own, e.g.

h *When he found some large bushes,* Tarquin drank his ginger beer *until he finally fell asleep, because he had become so bloated.*

Here we have three dependent clauses in italics and one independent clause. What's more, we can see that the independent clause is the indispensable one. You can remove any or all of the dependent clauses, but you can't remove the independent clause 'Tarquin drank his ginger beer' without destroying the structure and meaning of the whole sentence. The clauses in a complex sentence, unlike those in a compound sentence, are clearly *not* of equal importance. It is the independent clause that represents the core structure. To summarise, we can say that a complex sentence consists of one independent clause and one or more dependent clauses. If we give a lower case (i.e. small) letter to each dependent clause, we can see something of the variety that theoretically now becomes possible: **A** + **a** + **b** + **c** + etc.; **a** + **A** + **b** + **c** + etc.; and so on. Even in **h** the clause structure **a** + **A** + **b** + **c** could be altered to **A** + **a** + **b** + **c**. (Try it!) The position of the independent clause is potentially very flexible. And it doesn't end there!

We've seen that the compound sentence is actually restricted in that every one of its clauses has to contain a finite verb. This restriction doesn't apply to the dependent clauses of the complex sentence, so allowing far more variation in structure. Let's try redrafting **f**:

i *Finding some large bushes,* Tarquin drank his ginger beer.

Here the dependent clause is elliptical in that it omits the subject 'he' and contains the non-finite verb 'Finding' instead of the finite 'found'. That's the grammatical difference between **f** and **i**, but there's also a resulting difference in emphasis. In **i** there's a perceptibly stronger emphasis on Tarquin and his action in drinking the ginger beer than there is in **f**. This is achieved by the unequal balancing of the two clauses, one having the non-finite verb 'Finding' and the other the finite verb 'drank', as opposed to both having the finite verbs 'found' and 'drank'. We can now sense something of the shades of meaning possible by the manipulation of grammatical constructions. Just before we return to *The BFG*, let's play around with **h** a little more:

j *Finding some large bushes,* Tarquin drank his ginger beer *until, becoming so bloated, he finally fell asleep.*

The structure of **h** and **j** is the same in terms of dependent and independent clauses (**a** + **A** + **b** + **c**), but the balance in emphasis has changed. In **h** the three dependent clauses are roughly similar in weight as they each contain a finite verb ('found', 'fell', 'had become'), whereas in **j** the clause 'until . . . he finally fell asleep' now seems more important than the other two dependent clauses as these now contain only non-finite verbs ('Finding' and 'becoming'). Notice also how the relative importance of 'becoming so bloated' is lessened by being placed *inside* another clause.

More complicated kinds of sentence build upon the basic patterns described here.

Some other grammar books refer to the independent clause as the **main clause**, and the dependent clause as the **subordinate clause**. The terms are completely interchangeable, but for consistency this book will continue to use the terms 'independent' and 'dependent'. And what of the words used to link the various dependent clauses – the 'When', 'until' and 'because' in **h** for example? Once again you'll find several names, but they're now usually called **subordinators**, because they introduce subordinate (what we're calling dependent) clauses. In particular, they introduce clauses concerned with time (e.g. 'before', 'after', 'when', 'while'), place (e.g. 'where'), reason (e.g. 'because', 'since'), purpose (e.g. 'so as to'), result (e.g. 'so that', 'until') and condition (e.g. 'although', 'if', 'unless', 'until').

If you're now ready to put this knowledge to the test, here's a short exercise on Text 13. Alternatively, you can continue to read on to the end of this section on kinds of sentence, and then choose Activity 19 or 20 (or both!) in order to test your understanding more fully.

ACTIVITY 18

1 In pairs, re-examine Text 13; you should have little difficulty in locating the one complex sentence. Now rewrite the passage by converting it into a number of complex sentences. (For example: 'Sophie couldn't sleep because a brilliant moonbeam, shining right on to her pillow, was slanting through a gap in the curtains.') Remember that each complex sentence can contain only one independent clause, though you can re-order the clauses as you wish.

2 In groups, compare your rewritten passages. How many different versions have been produced? Discuss whether any of them might be suitable as introductions to the book, and whether you think the age range of the target audience would be affected.

Ever increasing spirals ...

Though extremely useful, subordinators are not the only means of introducing dependent clauses. One especially common type of dependent clause is the **relative clause**, a clause that adds further information about someone or something just mentioned. It's introduced by what's called a **relative pronoun**: a word (e.g. 'who', 'that', or 'which') that *relates* back to the person or thing about to be described. Here's a sentence containing two (italicised) relative clauses:

k Romulus, *who was a glutton*, ate all the maple syrup pancakes *that were on the table.*

You can see that **k** is simply a variation of the complex sentence, containing one independent clause 'Romulus ate all the maple syrup pancakes' and two dependent clauses 'who was a glutton' and 'that were on the table'. The relative clause is just a very useful form of the dependent clause.

To complete our rapidly growing appreciation of overall structure, we need to consider the method of increasing the length and variety of sentences still more. The resulting **compound-complex sentence** may sound a bit of a mouthful, but it's actually no more than a combination of the essential elements we've just examined in the compound sentence and the complex sentence. In other words it must contain at least two independent clauses (that's the compound part) and at least one dependent clause (the complex part). Here's a straightforward example with the dependent clause italicised:

1 *Although they were both bloated,* Tarquin drank more ginger beer and Romulus ate more maple syrup pancakes.

And if you wished you could add any number of further dependent clauses describing when, where and why the pair continued to indulge themselves. *Any* number? Well, we'll see about that shortly. First it might be helpful to summarise all this structural information in a table for reference:

Sentence	Definition	Example
Minor	An incomplete clause	Finding a sword.
Simple	One independent clause	Xena struck the barbarian.
Multiple (3 kinds):	Two or more clauses:	
Compound	Two or more independent clauses	Xena struck the barbarian and severed his big toe.
Complex	One independent clause + one or more dependent clauses	Finding a sword, Xena struck the barbarian.
Compound-Complex	Two or more independent clauses + one or more dependent clauses	Finding a sword, Zena struck the barbarian and severed his big toe.

And there you have the basic template for sentence structure! The clauses can vary in form, function and sequence; the links between them can be equally diverse. However, none of this grammatical knowledge is of much use by itself; you need to make it work for you by applying it to actual texts. The challenge now is to use this information to analyse the structural choices made by writers, and to appreciate the effect that these choices have on meaning.

ACTIVITY 19

1 Turn back to Text 12 in chapter 2. (Your notes from Activity 14, though not essential, would be useful.) In pairs, analyse the seven sentences into the various kinds that you're now familiar with (simple, compound, etc.). Which kind is not represented in the passage?

2 In small groups, compare and agree your analysis. Hemingway has been criticised by some for his unvaried and repetitive sentence structure. From this admittedly short sample, discuss what grammatical characteristics you think contribute to his particular style, i.e. his 'stylistic fingerprints'.

3 In pairs or small groups, rewrite the passage using a different choice of sentence structures. You should as far as possible retain the wording of the original.
4 As a class, discuss the possible reasons for Hemingway's own choices.
5 Alternatively, if you did not choose Activity 18 earlier, you should apply the same general procedure to Text 13 as follows. In pairs, analyse this text into its various kinds of sentence. Then discuss any characteristic pattern you detect as part of Dahl's technique, rewrite the passage with a different choice of sentence structure and finally assess the effect.

As a further alternative, here's another extract from a children's book, this time aimed at a slightly older readership. It's part of the introductory chapter to JK Rowling's *Harry Potter and the Chamber of Secrets*.

TEXT 14

[1]Harry looked nothing like the rest of the family. [2]Uncle Vernon was large and neckless, with an enormous black moustache; Aunt Petunia was horse-faced and boney; Dudley was blond, pink and porky. [3]Harry, on the other hand, was small and skinny, with brilliant green eyes and jet black hair that was always untidy. [4]He wore round glasses, and on his forehead was a thin, lightning-shaped scar.

[5]It was this scar that made Harry so particularly unusual, even for a wizard. [6]This scar was the only hint of Harry's very mysterious past, of the reason he had been left on the Dursleys' doorstep eleven years before.

[7]At the age of one, Harry had somehow survived a curse from the greatest dark sorcerer of all time, Lord Voldemort, whose name most witches and wizards still feared to speak. [8]Harry's parents had died in Voldemort's attack, but Harry had escaped with his lightning scar, and somehow – nobody understood why – Voldemort's powers had been destroyed the instant he had failed to kill Harry.

[9]So Harry had been brought up by his dead mother's sister and her husband. [10]He had spent ten years with the Dursleys, never understanding why he kept making odd things happen without meaning to, believing the Dursleys' story that he had got his scar in the car crash which had killed his parents.

ACTIVITY 20

1 On your own, analyse the ten sentences in Text 14 into the kinds of sentence explained earlier (simple, compound, complex and compound-complex). Identify the number and sequence of the various clauses in each sentence. You may find it helpful to label each clause with an upper or lower case letter for ease of comparison between sentences. Again, don't worry about the odd sentence you may be unsure about; concentrate on those whose pattern you recognise.
2 In small groups, compare your findings and discuss any particular difficulties. In what ways are Rowling's sentences different from Dahl's in Text 13? How do these differences reflect the distinct readership of each?

... or circles?

Just how long can a sentence stretch? Texts like *The BFG* might lead us to believe that young children can't cope with lengthy sentences, but we've only to look at such nursery rhymes as *The House that Jack Built* to realise this just isn't true. Here's the final verse of one traditional version:

TEXT 15

This is the farmer sowing his corn,

That kept the cock that crowed in the morn,

That waked the priest all shaven and shorn,

That married the man all tattered and torn,

That milked the cow with the crumpled horn,

That tossed the dog,

That worried the cat,

That killed the rat,

That ate the malt,

That lay in the house that Jack built.

ACTIVITY 21

1 As a group or class, discuss what features assist in the comprehension of this one sentence. How much further do you think such a sentence could be extended and yet remain acceptable to its target audience?

2 In pairs, choose a genre of writing (e.g. the fairy tale) and write an opening simple sentence that can be extended. Each pair should then pass this sentence on to the next pair, who should add a dependent clause and then pass it on again (e.g. 'There was once a handsome prince, who was out riding one morning, when he saw a lovely maiden, who . . .' etc.) You can keep on passing your texts around until exhaustion sets in. A person from each pair should then read out one of the final versions. At what point in each text does the sentence break down? Why?

Read the commentary at the end of this chapter, then read on.

Legal circles

In practice, then, words in sentences can't spiral away endlessly, not because of any grammatical constraint, but because of a human constraint. At some point the words must come full circle and close with a full stop. But how do you account for the following text?

TEXT 16

> (2) If, in a case where this subsection applies, it appears to the rent tribunal, on an application made by the lessor for a direction under this section, –
>
> (a) that the lessee has not complied with the terms of the contract, or
>
> (b) that the lessee or any person residing or lodging with him has been guilty of conduct which is a nuisance or annoyance to adjoining occupiers or has been convicted of using the dwelling, or allowing the dwelling to be used, for an immoral or illegal purpose, or
>
> (c) that the condition of the dwelling has deteriorated owing to any act or neglect of the lessee or any person residing or lodging with him, or
>
> (d) that the condition of any furniture provided for the use of the lessee under the contract has deteriorated owing to any ill-treatment by the lessee or any person residing or lodging with him,
>
> the rent tribunal may direct that the period referred to in subsection (1) above shall be reduced so as to end at a date specified in the direction.

This text is a short and fairly straightforward (yes!) sentence from a legal statute: section 106 (2) of the *Rent Act 1977*. Lacking legal training, we may find it virtually incomprehensible, and it's the complicated grammatical structure that intensifies the problem. We seem to go round and round in circles, without any increase in understanding. But there is a deliberate pattern here, though one unusual to all but members of the legal profession.

ACTIVITY 22

1 In small groups, re-read Text 16. How many different kinds of grammatical structure can you identify as recurring within the text? To help unravel the sentence pattern, look for the relative pronouns and subordinators.

2 What other features make the structure of the sentence unusual?

3 As a class, share your findings and reach agreement on the significant stylistic features of the text. Were you able to detect the subject of the independent clause?

You should now read the commentary on this Activity at the end of the chapter.

The rather convoluted patterns in Text 16 typify some of the ways in which legal statutes are drafted. In fact, these statutes are recognisable as much by their structures as by their vocabulary. You may already be familiar with the term **collocation** (literally a 'placing together'), referring to the way in which words share a greater or lesser tendency to occur together. Certain words go together more frequently, and this causes their collocation to become more predictable. For example, the phrases 'fish and chips' and 'peaches and cream', the word 'boggle' with 'eye' or 'mind', or in a larger context, words like 'prince', 'princess', 'dragon', and 'witch' in a fairy tale. Likewise, in the context of the law on rent, we might predict that words such as 'lessor', 'lessee', 'rent tribunal' and 'dwelling' are highly likely to collocate. Collocation is of course a lexical concept, because it relates to the choice of words, but there is a corresponding grammatical concept.

Many texts are also recognisable by the grammatical structures that predominate within them. We've already seen that this is true of legal statutes. **Colligation** (literally a 'binding together') is the term that refers to the ways in which words are tied together in structural patterns. As you progress through this book you'll increase your knowledge of these patterns, but for the moment we can say that statute law, as a specific genre, is recognisable as much by its typical colligations as by its predictable collocations.

Sentences for dummies . . .

Before we continue, we need to tie up a few loose ends in our strings of words. This introductory book can't possibly examine all the exceptions and oddities in grammar, but on the other hand, if it's to be of any real use, it must deal with some of the more common ones that you're likely to encounter in everyday texts. So, now that you've mastered basic sentence structure, let's briefly return to the simple sentence. You'll have no trouble in recognising these basic patterns:

m Ariadne is a first-rate escapologist. (SVC)
n Ariadne escaped. (SV)
o Ariadne escaped her pursuers. (SVO)

But what about

p It's Ariadne.

Intuitively, you probably feel it's complete, and you can easily imagine contexts in which it could be uttered, for example by someone seeing her enter the room. Grammatically, it contains a finite copular verb 'is', and if you apply the two-stage method of identifying a subject, you arrive at 'It'. But this does seem a bit odd. For on the one hand, if you reverse **m** you get

q A first-rate escapologist is Ariadne. (SVC)

which is unusual but acceptable, and retains the essential meaning. (It's more colloquial and it emphasises Ariadne's skill.) But if you reverse **p** you get

r Ariadne's it.

which might conceivably be possible (e.g. in a game of tag), but doesn't seem to mean the same thing at all. 'It' obviously refers to Ariadne, but what does 'It' actually mean? You could ask the same question of any number of everyday utterances like 'It's snowing' or 'It's nice to come home'. In each case 'It' seems unnecessary, for what we mean is something like 'Snow is falling' or 'To come home is nice'. So why don't we just say this?

The answer is related to the way our minds normally process information. Generally, sentences begin with what the listener or reader already knows and then add information that the listener or reader doesn't know. This relationship is referred to as the **Given/New Contract**. Sentences don't usually occur in isolation; they follow one another and are consequently related to one another in meaning. It's much easier for the listener or reader to understand and follow a conversation or text if the starting point of each sentence refers to something known or previously mentioned. (Look back, for instance, at Text 12 on page 26.) The subject of a sentence usually appears at or near the beginning of a sentence (remember SVO?), and it also usually refers to something already known by the listener or reader. So in order to preserve the normal SVO or SVC structure, and postpone the communication of the new element (e.g. the snowing, the niceness of coming home, or Ariadne), we create an artificial subject that effectively acts as a signal that something new is about to be reported. If a speaker or writer doesn't follow this pattern, then the immediate emphasis on the new information is likely to come across as more significant or emotive (e.g. 'Snow is here' or 'Nice to come home, isn't it?'). The 'It' as a subject is referred to as a **dummy subject**, because many linguists consider the 'It' to be a purely artificial contrivance with no meaning. Yet arguably its use does convey a meaning, often an attitude of less personal involvement than the alternative grammatical structures available.

ACTIVITY 23

1 In small groups, turn back to Text 6 on page 15. The word 'it' occurs as a subject four times in the passage. For each occurrence, identify what exactly 'it' refers to. Are there any examples of a dummy subject?

2 As a class discuss and agree your analysis of the relevant subjects.

... but is there a dummy?

Another common construction is the 'There + copular verb', e.g.:

s   There's an escapologist in town.

Actually, you've seen other examples earlier in this book:

t   There was a peculiar similarity between himself and his wife. (Text 11)
u   There were two flying fish inside. (Text 12)

If you undertook Activity 14, how did you analyse these two sentences? AVS possibly? If so, that's fine. Yet some linguists argue (well, they would!) that 'There' is another instance of a dummy subject, for the same reason that 'It' often is. Certainly, 'There' doesn't always appear to relate to a particular place or even time, and its meaning isn't constant in the three sentences **s** to **u**.

A word of reassurance may be needed here! You'll have realised that the dummy subject sentence is an extremely common kind of construction, especially in speech; it's therefore one that you'll want to feel confident in examining. But it's also a conventional or formulaic structure of a rather elementary sort. At this stage it's simplest to think of it as a basic SV opening structure, and then concentrate your analysis upon the relative simplicity or complexity of whatever is added to it. You don't have to hyperventilate over the issue of what function 'There' actually performs! However, for those who are interested . . .

ACTIVITY 24

1 In groups of two or three, rewrite sentences **s** to **u** by omitting the word 'There'. Discuss any differences you detect in emphasis or meaning. What's the effect of replacing 'in town' in **s** and 'inside' in **u** by 'there'?

2 As a class, discuss why you think some linguists prefer the analysis SVC to AVS (or AVC) for sentences like these. (Clue: you might consider what you've already learnt about the basic structure of the English sentence.) You should also consider sentence 8 in Text 11 (page 26).

There is a short commentary on this Activity at the end of the chapter.

The following passage is from *Weather Watch* by Dick File, a book that aims to explain the nature of weather to the interested general reader. Here are the opening two paragraphs on tornadoes.

TEXT 17

[1]A tornado is a rapidly rotating column of air. [2]It is a violent phenomenon despite its small scale, but is generally short-lived, usually lasting less than an hour. [3]During its brief life a tornado will wreak destruction along its path in a swathe perhaps 100 m (300 ft) across and a few kilometres in length. [4]Despite dramatic pictures of wrecked buildings in the USA, the main damage is to crops. [5]Dark clouds and heavy rain are nearby when the tornado is first spotted. [6]It may be visible as a blackish column hanging from a cloud, sometimes narrowing towards the ground, or at a later stage in its life as a rope-like twisted feature apparently connecting the cloud to the surface. [7]Sometimes this connection may be broken temporarily as the vortex lifts away from the ground only to return a few minutes later, but more often this is the sign of decay.

[8]The cause of the tornado is certainly linked with the formation of large, rapidly developing cumulonimbus clouds. [9]Lightning, thunder and hail may well occur simultaneously. [10]Though imprecisely understood, it seems that the huge upcurrent in the storm starts rotating and this induces the funnel cloud at the base of the storm. [11]Pressure is very low in the middle of a tornado, as can be inferred from the damage, which is due to a combination of suction and strong winds. [12]Wind speeds as high as 280 mph (450 kph) were ascribed to a tornado in Texas in April, 1958. [13]The fact that 'twisters' rotate anticlockwise in the northern hemisphere is proof that they are large enough systems to be affected by the Earth's rotation (the Coriolis effect again). [14]Descriptions and photographs of tornadoes rotating in the 'wrong' direction are not wholly convincing, because it is so easy to be misled when watching flying debris.

ACTIVITY 25

1 Individually prepare a detailed analysis of Text 17, identifying:
   (a) the kinds of sentence that occur (e.g. simple, complex, and so on),
   (b) the number of clauses in each sentence and their type (e.g. independent, dependent finite, dependent non-finite),
   (c) the varied sequence of these clauses.

2 In small groups, compare your analyses and reach agreement over any differences. Now locate the first independent clause of each sentence and examine the subject. How are these subjects related to one another?

3 Next examine the sequence of clauses in each sentence. To what extent does the subject of each refer to or rely upon the 'Given' (i.e. something already known or previously identified), and the verb phrase supply the 'New' (i.e. something not known)?

4 In larger groups or as a class, compare your findings and discuss how the structure of this passage is suited to the communication of its meaning.

Read the commentary on this Activity at the end of the chapter carefully. Then read on.

Sentence types

We'll end this chapter with something that you may well be familiar with already, but that you'll now be in a better position to appreciate: the four types of sentence. We've already classified sentences into different degrees of complexity, but now we're looking at another aspect: how do different grammatical forms of a sentence reflect the different basic functions that they perform? By far the most common type of sentence is the **declarative**, which 'declares' or makes a statement that something is or isn't so. Next comes the **interrogative**, which asks a question about whether something is so; then the **imperative**, which commands or demands that someone do something; and finally the **exclamative**, which expresses a strong emotional response. Some simple examples:

v   Ariadne is a brilliant escapologist.   (Declarative)
w   Is Ariadne a brilliant escapologist?   (Interrogative)
x   Escape from that.   (Imperative)
y   What a brilliant escape!   (Exclamative)

These four types can actually perform other functions, but that complication would take us away from grammar and into **pragmatics**, a different aspect of language altogether. So let's stick with the purely grammatical definition for the moment: declaratives state, interrogatives ask, imperatives command and exclamatives exclaim!

ACTIVITY 26

1 In small groups, examine the four sentences **v** to **y**. The last two don't include all the essential parts that we'd earlier decided must appear in a sentence if it's to be grammatically complete. Which parts are missing from each?

2 Now make up your own examples of imperatives and exclamatives that include various combinations of the components S, V, O and C.

3 In larger groups or as a class, compare your examples. What can you say about the normal patterns possible for these two sentence types? Which component would be highly unusual in an imperative? And why?

You should read the commentary at the end of the chapter before continuing.

Weaving another pattern

Because the declarative is by far the most common sentence type, you should always note the appearance of the other types, and ask yourself why they're there. The potential for mixing sentence types is one more strand in the intricate patterning of texts. We'll end with the first section of a combined leaflet and mail order form, aimed at the Australian general public to promote a product.

TEXT 18

EMU OIL INFORMATION

THE HAYMAN PRODUCE & EMU FARM
Lot 2 Warrego Highway, MARBURG. Q.4346. (P.O. Box 52 MARBURG)
Ph:- 07 54644667 Fax:- 07 54644057 Mobile:- 0412 884931
Info@HaymanEMU.com.au   www.HaymanEMU.com.au

EMU OIL:- Emu Oil has natural, therapeutic, penetrating and anti-inflammatory properties. Emu Oil is a natural source of Vitamins A and E. These qualities make it an ideal moisturiser. Emu Oil is also a natural source of Omega 3, 6 and 9 oils and contains 10 fatty acids which are great for your health.

ARTHRITIS, JOINT & MUSCULAR PROBLEMS:- The penetrating qualities of emu oil help lubricate the joint and the anti-inflammatory properties help reduce the swelling and relieve pain. Rub emu oil into the affected area 3 to 4 times a day. It will take several days to penetrate into the joint. Emu oil reduces the swelling in sprain and ligament damage. Try it on bruising, tendons and other aches and pains.

SKIN PROBLEMS:- Try emu oil on tinea, ezcema, dermatitis, psoriasis and nappy rash. Emu oil helps relieve the itchiness and redness associated with these skin problems. The natural vitamins in emu oil help the skin to heal. Apply pure emu oil to affected area 2–4 times a day.

CUTS & ABRASIONS, BURNS, SUNBURN & BLISTERS:- Emu oil speeds up the healing process and reduces scarring. The natural vitamins help soothe and moisturize burns and sunburn. Apply emu oil to a CLEAN wound. Emu oil applied to blisters disperses the fluid and helps the skin to heal. Try our Hand & Body Lotion on sunburn. Apply oil 2 or 3 times a day.

INSECT BITES:- The natural anti-inflammatory properties in emu oil relieve itching and help bites to heal. Apply oil every few hours if possible. Emu oil applied to the skin helps stop midges and sandflies from biting.

EAR INFECTIONS:- Emu oil reduces the inflammation associated with ear aches. Apply 1 or 2 drops of emu oil into the ear twice a day for 2–3 days.

ACTIVITY 27

1 In small groups, count and identify the sentence types in Text 18. Discuss why these types have been chosen in this proportion and what effects they attempt to achieve. Could other sentence types have been used? If so, what different effects might have been achieved, and how would altering the relative proportion of each type be a significant factor?

2 Examine the sentence structures in terms of their clause structure and their separate components (i.e. S, V, O, C and A). How complicated and varied are they? What grammatical patterns can you detect?

3 If time permits, you should also examine the subjects of each sentence, and the relative provision of given and new information in their sequence.

4 Summarise your findings, so that a spokesperson from each group can report back to the class. Discuss and agree the specific colligations that this text displays.

You might expect that some genres would naturally use predominantly one sentence type. For example, that the informative textbook would use declaratives (see Text 16), or that the recipe would use imperatives. But how true is this?

ACTIVITY 28

1 Individually, during the next week, collect as many different kinds of text as you can. Choose a section from each, and count up the number of each sentence type. Do the texts contain the types you would have predicted, or are some unexpected? (Looking at examples of the same kind of text aimed at different audiences can be instructive, e.g. a non-fiction book aimed at young children, older children, and adults. Alternatively, you might search out different examples of a specific genre, such as the information leaflet.)

2 Write up your findings as a short report on the types of text you chose and the discoveries you made, or alternatively bring your texts to class for a general discussion.

COMMENTARY
On Activity 16

The verb groups in each sentence are:

1	couldn't sleep	**9**	was
2	was slanting	**10**	came
3	was shining	**11**	were
4	had been	**12**	was; was walking
5	closed; lay	**13**	went
6	tried . . . to doze	**14**	could be heard
7	was	**15**	had . . . known
8	was; slicing		

The three sentences that aren't simple are 5, 8 and 12. Sentence 5 contains two finite verbs ('closed' and 'lay'); sentence 8 contains the finite verb 'was' and the non-finite participle 'slicing' as separate verb groups; sentence 12 again contains two finite verbs in separate verb groups ('was' and 'was walking'). Notice also that other types of word can be inserted within a verb group: 'very hard' in sentence 6; 'never' in sentence 15. (Some linguists would also argue that the negative '-n't' attached to 'could' in sentence 1 is not strictly part of the verb group, but you needn't worry about such detailed analysis!)

COMMENTARY
On Activity 21

Some of the grammatical (as opposed to semantic) features you should have identified in the nursery rhyme are:

- the repetition of a dependent clause introduced by the relative pronoun 'that'
- the similarity in structure in that most clauses contain a finite verb in the past tense followed by a direct object, e.g. 'kept the cock', 'waked the priest'.

This nursery rhyme demonstrates **recursion**, a term used to refer to any repeated grammatical structure. *Theoretically*, such structures can be repeated endlessly, without upsetting the essentially correct grammatical nature of the sentence. However, in practice you'll have found that there are limits to your capacity for processing such structures, in terms of both your understanding and your memory. You might like to count how many clauses (and words) there were in the longest *acceptable* sentence that you were able to create in pairs. You'll also have realised that prolonged recursion doesn't offer a very interesting method for developing the sentence.

COMMENTARY

On Activity 22

Not an easy exercise, but you should have found that you weren't as severely handicapped by your lack of specialist legal knowledge as you might at first have imagined. Some recurring grammatical structures you should have noticed are:

- relative clauses (of varying complexity), the more important ones beginning with 'that'
- use of dependent clauses with non-finite verbs (e.g. 'residing or lodging with him')
- pairs of nouns, verbs, etc. linked with the coordinator 'or' (e.g. 'nuisance or annoyance', 'act or neglect', 'residing or lodging')
- the high number of adverbials occurring at intervals throughout the sentence.

Clearly there is a more varied form of recursion here. Some of the other features you should have noticed include:

- the lack of ellipsis and the consequent repetition of words and phrases
- the layout of the sentence, including the lettering of the most important relative clauses
- although a lengthy complex sentence, its one independent clause occurs almost at the very end ('the rent tribunal may direct').

This marked use of repetition and recursion helps identify the text as a piece of specialist legal drafting. The language of the law strives to be unambiguously clear and exact. It uses these grammatical features to help achieve this, and so produces sentences that are self-contained in their reference. The grammatical patterns are there to *assist* comprehension, and so form an integral part of the text's meaning.

COMMENTARY

On Activity 24

Some of the relevant issues that you should have discussed are:

- a major sentence must contain both S and V
- the normal order for these components in English is SV
- 'There + copular verb' (see page 24) is a very common construction
- the copular verb is normally followed by C not S
- 'There' frequently doesn't refer to a place or time.

You'll have realised that an AVS or AVC analysis for such a commonly occurring construction would conflict with the recognised normal pattern of SVO or SVC in the English language. There's no definitive solution to this debate, but you might finally like to consider whether the analysis SVC is prescriptive or descriptive.

COMMENTARY

On Activity 25

Again not an easy exercise in places, but one in which you should have been able to make *some* useful discoveries about grammatical patterns. Remember that any 'real' text will display problems of grammatical analysis somewhere, but that's no reason to avoid the attempt. The kinds of sentence represented are:

Simple: six (sentences 1, 3, 4, 8, 9, 12)

Complex: five (sentences 5, 6, 11, 13, 14)

Compound-complex: three (sentences 2, 7, 10).

The majority of sentences contain between one and four clauses (sentences 10 and 14 are slightly more complicated – see postscript). Though there exists considerable variety in the patterning of finite and non-finite dependent clauses, only in sentence 10 is the first clause non-finite ('Though imprecisely understood'). All other sentences begin with an independent clause, thereby establishing and maintaining the central theme of the text. Relative emphasis on information is achieved by mixing finite and non-finite dependent clauses. Look, for instance, at the emphasis on the explanation contained in the two finite dependent clauses ('as can be . . . and strong winds') that follow the opening independent clause in sentence 11. Now compare these to the less emphatic treatment of the facts within the non-finite clause at the end of sentence 2 ('usually lasting less than an hour') or at the beginning of sentence 10 ('Though imprecisely understood').

The subject of the first independent clause in each sentence is:

Sentence	Subject
1	A tornado
2	It
3	a tornado
4	the main damage
5	Dark clouds and heavy rain
6	It
7	this connection
8	The cause of the tornado
9	Lightning, thunder and hail
10	it
11	Pressure
12	Wind speeds as high as 280 mph (450 kph)
13	The fact that 'twisters' rotate anticlockwise in the northern hemisphere
14	Descriptions and photographs of tornadoes rotating in the 'wrong' direction

The repetition or development of information contained in these grammatical subjects shows how the topic of the tornado is maintained clearly for the reader as additional facts are provided. Most of the subjects after sentence 1 refer to information that has been given or clearly implied. New information (e.g. in the subjects of sentences 5 and 11) is not so unrelated that it can't quickly be assimilated. And this careful grammatical construction is probably what you would expect of a text designed to describe and explain a particular event in the natural world to the non-specialist. Information has been selected and integrated into a unified passage, using particular colligations. The sentences are predominantly simple or complex, thereby containing just one independent clause to maintain the central theme of the passage. Yet there is also variety for the reader in that no more than two sentences of the same kind ever occur consecutively. When we examine the ways in which a text is made into a unified whole, we speak of its **cohesion**. Cohesion (literally a 'sticking together') can be achieved by various means including lexical collocation, phonological or graphological devices, and grammatical patterning (i.e. colligation). We'll return to this matter of grammatical cohesion later (page 91).

Postscript: If you encountered some difficulty or uncertainty in analysing sentences 10 and 14, don't be disheartened! Both sentences contain the dummy subject 'it', which complicates their structure. However, you might like to refer again to the discussion of this topic on page 42, and then re-examine the two sentences. Why has the dummy been used, and what happens if you rewrite the sentences without it (e.g. in 10: 'the huge upcurrent in the storm seems to start rotating')?

COMMENTARY
On Activity 26

You should have discovered that the imperative sentence can occur as V, as VO or as VC, but that its subject (normally 'You', whether singular or plural) is not usually mentioned, because the context would make perfectly clear who is being addressed. You can recognise an imperative sentence not only because the verb appears at the beginning, but also because it always occurs in its basic form – it's always the infinitive minus 'to' (see page 17). However, for purposes of emphasis it is possible to mention the subject, e.g.

y   *Ariadne*, escape!
z   *You*, come here!

though you can see that the effect is often to make the imperative double up, so to speak, as an exclamation. Which leads us neatly to a comment on the exclamative. You should have discovered that exclamatives are incredibly flexible and can be expressed by any combination of components. They don't require an explicit subject or verb, though they may include one or both. In practice, they're usually minor rather than major sentences, the reason being that emotional expression is more forceful (and perhaps natural) when it's elliptical. You should also have discovered that declaratives, interrogatives and imperatives can function simultaneously as exclamatives.

Summary

In this chapter you have:

- investigated in detail the structure of the sentence
- discovered the distinct patterning in specific types of text
- developed your skills of grammatical analysis.

4 Grammar and Nonsense!

In this chapter you will:

- explore the two main types of word in English
- divide words into a number of different classes
- distinguish between form and function in language
- examine the noun phrase in some depth.

Nice grammar, shame about the sense

Authors have often deliberately created new and unusual words to achieve special effects. Some of these words were never intended to have much actual meaning (e.g. the invented words in the humorous verse of Lewis Carroll and Edward Lear, or the mock dialect of Stella Gibbons in her comic novel *Cold Comfort Farm*). Others were intended to communicate meaning within the language of a futuristic society (e.g. the teenage slang in *A Clockwork Orange* by Anthony Burgess). Here's the opening of a short nonsense story, *The Prampsy Grindler* by Vera Shutka. The italicised words have been invented by the author to suggest . . . well, do you feel prampsy?

TEXT 19

[1]There was once a *prampsy grindler* who *stompled* from *grilt* to *glot* in his *jandamest*. [2]He was very *ulpsome*, and would *frimp gloopsily* or even *armestically*. [3]Oh how he *frimped*, till *tugglebobs* would *crimble* down his *vardy arples*! [4]But there were *prampsier esterflops* under the *trepangle*, and these had to be *maldicated* most *nebrily* with *mershy brish*.

ACTIVITY 29

1 In small groups, read Text 19. It's not possible, of course, to work out the meaning of the italicised words, as they're deliberately nonsensical. However, it *is* possible to replace each one by a genuine word that does have meaning.

2 Rewrite the story, substituting a real word for each nonsense word, so that the story makes consistent sense.

3 As a class, compare your completed stories. It's unlikely that they will resemble one another! But now take each nonsense word in turn and list all the words substituted for it. In each case do you detect any similarity among the words, not in the meaning but in the *kind* of word, e.g. noun or verb?

4 Wherever there is agreement on the kind of word, you should discuss how it is that groups working independently have nevertheless achieved this. Can it be coincidental? Be as specific as possible about the likely reasons.

Before you read on, you should read the comprehensive commentary on this activity at the end of the chapter.

We'll need to summarise and assess these findings before we continue. Let's start with a seemingly easy question. What is a sentence made of? A short while ago you might well have replied, 'Words, of course. What else?' Though perfectly true, this answer isn't actually very useful. But this Activity has shown you something very significant: sentences are composed not simply of words, but of groups of words, and these groups of words form recurring patterns. You also recognise these patterns intuitively, *even if you don't understand the meaning*; otherwise you wouldn't have been able to complete the Activity successfully! These various patterns demonstrate that there are a number of rules for combining words in meaningful chunks. The rules are in your head, though not necessarily at a conscious level, and certainly not with any attached grammatical terminology! Native speakers possess an unconscious knowledge of the grammatical rules of their language – a **linguistic competence** – that enables them to speak it and understand it. Learning the appropriate grammatical terms will make you more aware of these rules and of the choices speakers and writers make. In fact, as you're fast becoming a specialist in the English language, you can't really afford not to know these terms!

The four classes of word we've identified here (noun, verb, adjective and adverb), though they normally perform different jobs within the sentence, share one characteristic that distinguishes them from other classes of words. On their own they have definite meaning. In other words, if you're asked the meaning of any noun, verb, adjective or adverb that you know, you'll probably be able to supply a definition or explain the meaning. (Try it!) It may not be a perfect dictionary definition, but as a makeshift description it will probably do. Such words are called **content words**, because they contain clearly identifiable meaning. Their main purpose is to convey the essential meaning of the sentence.

ACTIVITY 30

1 In small groups, re-examine Text 19. Concentrate solely on the words that aren't in italics (but ignore the adverb 'once'). In what way do they differ significantly from the italicised words? (Clue: take your rewritten version and write out each sentence again, first with only your new content words and then with just the remaining words.)

2 As a class compare your observations. What seems to be the purpose of these words?

Read the commentary at the end of the chapter, then read on.

All words in English can be classified as either content or function. This division simply reflects the main purpose of the words: either to express meaning or to show grammatical relationships. The four word classes that together make up the content words can also be considered as open sets. In other words, new examples of nouns, verbs, adjectives and adverbs are created every day in order to express some new meaning, thereby increasing the size of the sets. Function words can also be subdivided into a number of separate classes, as we'll see shortly (page 54). However, these classes are closed sets and contain relatively few words. There's rarely any need for additions to these sets, as the words within them are extremely versatile in their capacity for constant reuse.

One thing may be puzzling you. You'll have noticed that earlier we included the verb as a class of content word, yet a little later we discussed 'was' and 'had' as examples of function words. This apparent contradiction is in fact quite easy to reconcile. You may remember that in Chapter 2 (page 16) we saw that a verb, because it's often composed of more than one word, is more sensibly called a verb group. If you take the sentence

a   Vesta built a rockery over her potato patch.

you can see that the verb 'built' is just one word that simultaneously expresses the meaning and indicates the past tense (when the action occurred – see page 15). But in the sentence

b   Vesta was building a rockery over her potato patch.

you can see that the verb group now comprises the two words 'was building'. The essential meaning of the particular action is contained in the last word of the group ('building'); the extra grammatical information about tense, number and person (that together makes the verb group finite) is contained in the word 'was'. We can say, then, that the last word in a verb group is a content word, because that's where the essential definable meaning lies, whereas any other words in the verb group are function words. The verb group can therefore be split in two. The content word that conveys the essential meaning is referred to as the **main verb** (or **lexical verb**); the one or more function words are referred to as the **auxiliary verbs**, because they perform an auxiliary or helping function by providing the essential grammatical information. Auxiliary verbs act to 'fine tune' the main verb. We'll return to these auxiliaries in Chapter 5 (page 78).

'Long time no viddy, droog.'

The following text is from *A Clockwork Orange* by Anthony Burgess. The novel is set in the future and is narrated by the main character, Alex, using 'nadsat', a teenage slang deliberately created by Burgess to indicate the futuristic setting. In this extract Alex, after failing to talk his way into someone's house, has left his friends outside and broken in upstairs.

TEXT 20

[1]So down I *ittied*, slow and gentle, admiring in the stairwell *grahzny* pictures of old time – *devotchkas* with long hair and high collars, the like country with trees and horses, the holy bearded *veck* all *nagoy* hanging on a cross. [2]There was a real musty *von* of pussies and pussy-fish and *starry* dust in this *domy*, different from the flatblocks. [3]And then I was downstairs and I could *viddy* the light in this front room where she had been doling *moloko* to the *kots* and *koshkas*. [4]More, I could *viddy* these great overstuffed *scoteenas* going in and out with their tales waving and like rubbing themselves on the door-bottom. [5]On a like big wooden chest in the dark hall I could *viddy* a nice *malenky* statue that shone in the light of the room, so I *crasted* this for my own self, it being like a young thin *devotchka* standing on one *noga* with her *rookers* out, and I could see this was made of silver. [6]So I had this when I *ittied* into the lit-up room, saying: 'Hi hi hi. [7]At last we meet. [8]Our brief *govoreet* through the letter-hole was not, shall we say, satisfactory, yes?'

1 In small groups, examine the italicised words, all examples of nadsat. Remember that these aren't nonsense words but have actual meaning. List the words and then try to identify as far as possible their intended meaning. The context provides clues, but some words are easier to decode than others.

2 Next, identify the class of word that each belongs to. You should examine the structure of each word as well as its relative position in the sentence. How does this help or reinforce your assessment of the meaning?

3 In larger groups or as a class, compare your findings, and discuss any words whose meaning you disagreed upon. Did you agree on the class of word in each case?

The commentary at the end of the chapter provides a key to this Activity.

The noun phrase is old hat

We're now going to examine a particularly important part of the sentence that's frequently made up of several word classes. You should be quite familiar with the noun, which we've described in some detail (page 64). However, nouns don't too often occur by themselves. They're far more likely to appear tied to one or more other words, a fact that has already helped you complete Activity 29. Let's try a simple experiment with a hat, or at least the word 'hat'. Any number of words could precede the word 'hat' in order to add details of various kinds. Here are just a few in no particular order:

red, cotton, pale, new, small, very, a, my, blue, splendid, big, silk, her, the, old, quite, dark, one, brilliant, leather.

1 In pairs or small groups, write out at least ten descriptions of the hat, using varied selections from the twenty given words. Use as many or as few as you like, but each time you can use any word only once, and you can't use any additional words. You'll quickly realise that some choices automatically prevent the use of other words.

2 Now examine your descriptions. Which words can't appear together?

3 Next examine the word order of your descriptions. How flexible are the word sequences? To what extent is the word order in each version interchangeable? Can you detect any recurring patterns in your examples?

4 In larger groups or as a class, compare your findings. Did any group produce a sequence that you think is grammatically unacceptable? Can you agree on any basic patterns in the sequence of possible words?

Read the commentary at the end of the chapter before reading on.

The one common element in every description was, of course, the word 'hat'. It's the key word without which the description is unrelated to an object. This key word, together with the group of connected words that surrounds it, is called the **noun phrase**. The key word itself, the noun, is referred to as the **head**, because any other words in the phrase are dependent on it. These other words are all **modifiers**, because they each add extra bits of information about the head. Before you begin to modify a noun, the potential for description seems infinite, but by choosing your first word you immediately reduce the remaining options. And the more words you choose to add, the more restricted those options become. These cumulative choices can be seen as creating a chain of words, the links of which form regular patterns with every added choice. You can try to lengthen this chain by using a recursive (see page 46) structure, e.g. 'a **very** old **very** red **very** splendid **very** attractive **very** fashionable ... etc. hat', but we've already seen that recursion can't be prolonged indefinitely (page 46). It was, of course, these chains of words that you were experimenting with during the last Activity.

The framework of English

Before we continue looking at the noun phrase, we need to identify the main classes of function words that provide the framework into which content words are placed. Linguists disagree over the exact number and names for these classes, but that needn't worry you. The vast majority of function words are included in one of the following six classes.

1 The **pronoun**. The pronoun is often erroneously defined as a word that stands in place of a noun. Occasionally this is true but more often it's not. A couple of examples will make the point. If in the sentence

c   Vesta is building a rockery.

we wish to replace the proper noun 'Vesta' by a pronoun, we get

d   *She* is building a rockery.

Fine. But if in the sentence

e   The young attractive gardener is building a rockery.

we once again replace only the common noun 'gardener' by a pronoun, we get

f   The young attractive *she* is building a rockery.

which clearly isn't acceptable. It now becomes apparent that the pronoun must stand for the complete noun phrase 'The young attractive gardener', not just the head word 'gardener'.

Pronouns are essential to efficient communication. They are a sort of shorthand reference, saving us the bother of repeating noun phrases every time we wish to refer to someone or something. As you can see from **f** you can't normally modify a pronoun with an adjective, and the pronoun itself replaces the noun phrase. But as is usual in grammatical matters, be prepared for exceptions (e.g. 'Poor you!'). Some of the main types of pronoun are:

- **Personal**
  (*I, me, you, he, him, she, her, we, us, they, them*) as in
  g   *We* must tell *them* to build a rockery.

- **Reflexive**
  (*myself, yourself, himself, herself, ourselves, yourselves, themselves, oneself*) as in

  h The happy gardeners sunned *themselves* in the rockery.

- **Possessive**
  (*mine, yours, his, hers, ours, theirs*) as in

  i *Yours* is in the rockery.

- **Relative** (see also page 36)
  (*who, which, that, whose*) as in

  j The gardener *who* built the rockery is attractive.

- **Interrogative**
  (*who? what? which? why? when? how?*) as in

  k *Who* is in the rockery?

- **Demonstrative**
  (*this, that, these, those*) as in

  l *Those* are in the rockery.

- **Indefinite**
  (*someone, no one, anybody, everything*)

A particular indefinite pronoun you should look out for is the so-called **impersonal** pronoun 'one', as in

m *One* should not misbehave in the rockery.

As its name suggests it's often used to refer to one or more persons rather formally, though it can also refer to an object, as in

n There are rocks in the rockery – take a small *one*.

You don't need to remember the names of the various types. It's far more important to appreciate how in each case the pronoun functions to replace a noun phrase. But you should notice how each type comprises a small number of very common – indispensable even – words.

2 The **determiner**. Generally speaking, the determiner precedes any adjective in a noun phrase. It supplies certain specific information about the head. The main types are:

- **Possessive**
  (*my, your, his, her, its, our, their, one's*) as in
  o *Your* beautiful rockery deserves a prize!

- **Demonstrative**
  (*this, that, these, those*) as in
  p *That* beautiful rockery deserves a prize.

- **Interrogative**
  (*which, what, whose*) as in
  q *Whose* beautiful rockery deserves a prize?

- **Quantifier**
  (e.g. *no, both, each, few, several, many, most, every, all*) as in
  r *Many* beautiful rockeries deserve prizes.

■ **Numeral**
(e.g. *one, two, three; first, second, third*) as in
s The **two** attractive gardeners have built their **seventh** beautiful
rockery.

But the commonest determiners by far are the **definite article** *the* and the
indefinite articles *a* (or *an*) and its plural form *some*, all of which are
among the most frequently used words in English.

3 The **connective**. The connective joins or links two chunks of language of
varying size: two words, phrases, clauses, sentences or even paragraphs.
Three main types are:

■ **Coordinator** (also called a **co-ordinating conjunction** – see page 33)
(e.g. *and, or, but, yet*) as in
t Ariadne *and* Vesta build rockeries together *yet* they always argue.

■ **Subordinator** (also called a **subordinating conjunction** – see page 36)
(e.g. *after, whenever, where, if, in case, because, since, though, unless, until*)
u Vesta builds rockeries *though* she quickly becomes tired.

■ **Conjunct** (see page 108)
Conjuncts tend to join larger units (not words or phrases), often making
clear the links between different stages in a story or argument.
(e.g. *however, nevertheless, meanwhile, next, therefore, now, consequently*)
v Vesta built a large rockery; *consequently* she felt very tired.

Once again, don't worry too much about these subdivisions. You just need
to appreciate the essential function of the connective in the framework of
the sentence.

4 The **preposition**. As its name suggests, the preposition is placed
('positioned') before ('pre') something else, usually a noun phrase. Its job is
to show how two parts of a sentence are related in terms of aspects such as
time or place. It's either one word or sometimes two or three words (rarely
more) that behave as if they were one. Some examples are:

One word:	*about, above, across, after, against, along, at, before, below, between, by, down, for, from, in, of, on, opposite, over, through, to, under, up, with.*
Two words:	*apart from, because of, close to, except for, far from, instead of, in to, near to, next to.*
Three words:	*as far as, in front of, in spite of, on behalf of.*

So for instance to show a relationship of time:

w *After* lunch, Vesta built three rockeries.

Or a relationship of place:

x Vesta placed cute garden gnomes *next to* the rockery.

Or some other relationship (in this case how something was done):

y Vesta built the rockery *with* the most beautiful stones.

Sentences **w** to **y** represent the typical pattern of a preposition followed by
a noun phrase:

Preposition	Noun phrase
After	lunch
next to	the rockery
with	the most beautiful stones

This combined structure of preposition plus noun phrase is called a **prepositional phrase**, because the preposition is the key word that governs or controls all the words that follow it within the noun phrase.

5 The **degree modifier** (or **intensifier**). This small class comprises words that were formerly classified as adverbs. In the past the adverb word class became a dumping ground for many words that couldn't easily be fitted into any other class. More recently, these words have been 'rescued' and given their own distinctive and more appropriate class. The degree modifier, as its name suggests, modifies or affects the word that follows it. More specifically, it shows the degree or extent to which the particular quality described in a following adjective or adverb exists. Some of the commonest degree modifiers are:

a bit, a little, approximately, exactly, extremely, fairly, more, most, quite, perfectly, rather, so, too, very.

They may modify an adjective, as in

z   The rockery was *very* beautiful.

or an adverb, as in

aa   Vesta built the rockery *very* quickly.

6 The **auxiliary verb**. You've already been introduced to auxiliary verbs in this chapter (page 52) and they're discussed in more detail later (page 78). The auxiliary verbs help out the meaning of the main verb by adding further information of various kinds. For example, differences in tense, number and person are conveyed by:

am, are, is, was, were, have, has, had, do, does, did.

Within those six classes you may have noticed that some names for specific types of function word, and indeed some actual words, occur more than once. For instance, **possessive** and **demonstrative** are types of pronoun *and* determiner, and they contain a number of the same words (e.g. *his, this, that*). However, after a moment's thought you'll realise that this isn't really a problem. Function words perform a number of different functions and are classified accordingly. Sometimes the same word can perform more than one function. You simply have to examine how the word relates to the others in the particular sentence in order to discover what type of function word it is. Words are only meaningful when they're related to other words; on their own many are actually unclassifiable. You cannot say whether the word 'which' on its own is a relative pronoun, an interrogative pronoun or an interrogative determiner, because on its own it isn't any of these. It simply has the *potential* to become any one of these, depending upon how it's used with other words. Some words can belong to several word classes. The word 'down' can be a noun, verb, adjective, adverb or preposition – check these in a dictionary! – and only its relation to surrounding words in a particular sentence will tell you which it is. A little practice in identifying word classes will therefore be useful before you progress further. The following text is a complete short story by R T Kurosaka called *A Lot To Learn*.

TEXT 21

The Materializer was completed.

Ned Quinn stood back, wiped his hands, and admired the huge bank of dials, lights and switches. Several years and many fortunes had gone into his project. Finally it was ready.

Ned placed the metal skullcap on his head and plugged the wires into the control panel. He turned the switch to ON and spoke: 'Pound note.'

There was a whirring sound. In the Receiver a piece of paper appeared. Ned inspected it. Real.

'Martini,' he said.

A whirring sound. A puddle formed in the Receiver. Ned cursed silently. He had a lot to learn.

'A bottle of beer,' he said.

The whirring sound was followed by the appearance of the familiar brown bottle. Ned tasted the contents and grinned.

Chuckling, he experimented further.

Ned enlarged the Receiver and prepared for his greatest experiment. He switched on the Materializer, took a deep breath and said, 'Girl.'

The whirring sound swelled and faded. In the Receiver stood a lovely girl. She was naked. Ned had not asked for clothing. She had freckles, a brace and pigtails. She was eight years old.

'Hell!' said Quinn.

Whirr.

The fireman found two charred skeletons in the smouldering rubble.

ACTIVITY 33

1 Individually, in preparation for a class, make an analysis of Text 21. You should first categorise the words as either content or function, then classify the content words into noun, main verb, adjective and adverb, and the function words into pronoun, determiner, connective, preposition, degree modifier and auxiliary verb. Make a careful note of any words you are unsure of.

2 In small groups in class, compare your analyses and reach agreement as far as possible. Now subdivide the word classes (e.g. nouns into proper and common; pronouns into personal, reflexive, possessive, etc). This is an excellent way of checking that your earlier classification into word classes was correct.

3 In larger groups or as a class discuss any 'problem' words. Why were there differences of opinion about them? Keep a note of any unresolved words.

More old hat!

If you attempted Activity 32 you'll now appreciate that the rules you discovered about acceptable and unacceptable sequences are clearly linked to the class of word preceding the noun. The words supplied were variously determiners, adjectives, and degree modifiers. Of course, you were perfectly able to sort them out without knowing those terms, but with those terms you can now more easily discuss their differences.

So, to return to Activity 32, you've placed half a dozen or more really striking modifiers in front of your noun, and by so doing you've exhausted your options for description. Or have you? Let's see.

bb a really brilliant green and purple cotton hat.

And then you have an afterthought – what about the yellow bobbles? No worries:

cc a really brilliant green and purple cotton hat with two yellow bobbles.

The answer is that you can extend the noun phrase *beyond* the head; the head isn't necessarily the end of the chain. However, the type of structure used after the head is noticeably different from that used before it. Whereas you might have said 'the yellow bobbly hat', you can't say 'the hat yellow bobbly'. In English, adjectives normally precede the head they relate to; they rarely follow, though there are different rules in some other languages. Instead, if you want to add information after the head, you normally have to use another structure, in this case a prepositional phrase (page 57) 'with two yellow bobbles'. You may have come up with some examples of description after the head when you worked on Activity 32, something like:

dd my very old red cotton hat – quite brilliant.

Such a pattern is natural in speech but uncommon in writing, and you'd certainly recognise this pattern as colloquial rather than formal. Your knowledge of what's usual allows you to notice the unusual.

Before and after

Your capacity for extra description is now greatly increased. Words may precede the head, follow the head, or indeed do both. This flexibility gives you far greater variety in your writing style, and also represents one of the many stylistic fingerprints to identify in other writers' work. Some linguists discriminate between the two types of modification by calling all words in the noun phrase that precede the noun **premodifiers**, and all those that follow the head **postmodifiers**. It can be a useful distinction, as we'll see. The noun phrase can expand in both directions rather like a concertina, and you can examine the relative balance and types of word that occur on each side of the head. There's also another advantage in using these two terms.

You've already seen that a word can belong to more than one class (page 57) and therefore needs other words around it before you can tell which class it belongs to in any particular sentence. In the commentary to Activity 32 we remarked that the three words 'cotton', 'silk' and 'leather' occurred immediately before the head. As isolated words they might at first appear to be nouns. After all, 'silky' or 'silken' for instance are clearly adjectives, but 'silk' doesn't perhaps immediately strike us as one. Faced with this puzzle older grammar books would describe 'silk' in the phrase 'silk hat' as a noun functioning as an adjective. This is somewhat confusing. How can a noun also be an adjective? The simplest way out of this dilemma is to define words according to how they group together or **colligate** (see page 41) in a sentence. If an apparent noun is actually modifying a head in a noun phrase, and is therefore clearly subordinate to it, then it's a premodifier in that noun phrase. So in the noun phrase 'a red silk hat' there are three premodifiers ('a' + 'red' + 'silk') followed by a head ('hat'). This use of the term premodifier neatly avoids the confusion of discussing nouns and adjectives. After all, both 'red' and 'silk' can be either, depending on how other words are grouped around them. We'll return to this matter later (page 63).

Form versus function: round 1 – in the red corner

At this point we're ready to make a very useful grammatical distinction that we'll return to again a little later in this chapter (page 63). If you take a simple sentence such as

ee The happy gardeners built a beautiful red sandstone rockery.

you can now analyse this in at least two separate ways. Firstly, it's plainly a typical SVO sentence:

S   V   O

ee The happy gardeners / built / a beautiful red sandstone rockery.

But secondly, if you examine the structure of the subject and object, you can now recognise that both are noun phrases. Furthermore, if you examine either noun phrase by itself, you can't tell whether it functions as a subject or an object. You obviously need to see the whole sentence. For example, the object in **ee** can just as easily function as a subject, as in

S   V   O

ff A beautiful red sandstone rockery / deserves / a prize.

Alternatively, the subject in **ee** can of course function as an object, as in

S   V   O

gg Everyone / admires / the happy gardeners.

As we saw earlier, the noun phrase is a particular category made up of certain types of word in certain predictable sequences. You therefore recognise it by its typical word pattern or colligation, in other words by the shape or *form* it appears in. But this word pattern can *function* in several ways, two of which are as a subject or as an object. **Form** and **function** are quite distinct aspects of language. The fact that some forms have several functions contributes to the variety and versatility of language. With this in mind, let's now examine some shorter texts.

The following two extracts are taken from a visitors' guide to Tambourine

Mountain in Queensland, Australia, and from *Sociology Themes and Perspectives*, an introductory textbook by Haralambos and Holborn.

TEXT 22

Tambourine Mountain, a volcanic plateau with a maximum length of eight kilometres and a width of five kilometres, 560 metres above sea level, is just thirty kilometres inland from Queensland's Gold Coast.

TEXT 23

The view of the USSR as a totalitarian society dominated by a ruling elite with absolute power, concerned primarily with furthering its own interests at the expense of the mass of the population, has been criticized by David Lane.

ACTIVITY 34

1 In pairs, identify the subject of the sentence in Texts 22 and 23. What general similarity do you notice about the subjects in relation to each complete sentence?

2 Rewrite the two sentences, altering them as little as possible, so that they seem more immediately understandable at a first reading.

3 In larger groups compare your findings and your versions.

Now read the short commentary at the end of this chapter on this Activity before reading on.

The text on the next page is the first part of a front-page story from *Eastern Eye*, a weekly tabloid newspaper aimed at the Asian community in the UK. The structure of the grammatical subjects is typical of tabloid journalism generally, but is quite distinctive when compared to other forms of writing. You now know enough about grammatical structure to discover what makes them unusual.

Generally, you should have found that each group chose a similar kind of word as follows:

Singular nouns:	grindler; jandamest; trepangle; brish.
Plural nouns:	tugglebobs; arples; esterflops.
Verbs:	stompled; frimp; frimped; crimble; maldicated.
Adjectives:	prampsy; ulpsome; vardy; prampsier; mershy.
Adverbs:	gloopsily; armestically; nebrily.

The remaining words, 'grilt' and 'glot', are more flexible, and depend on your earlier choice of verb for 'stompled'. Don't worry if you're unsure about the terms noun, adjective and adverb; we'll come to those. The things to check are:

■ Can you subdivide your choice of words into these groups?
■ Do the words in each group share any common features?

Words perform different jobs within a sentence and so are grouped into a number of **word classes** (what used to be called **parts of speech**) according to their particular function. Let's take a closer look at some of them.

First the noun. The **noun** as a particular class of word has often been defined as the name of a person, place or thing, but by itself this definition isn't sufficiently reliable or precise. Certainly nouns do refer to persons (judge, prince, escapologist), and to places (courtroom, country, seaside) and to things, whether physical objects (wig, beer, pancake) or concepts (justice, foolishness, truth). But this definition is concerned only with meaning – the semantic aspect. The structural or grammatical aspect is arguably far more important. How did you know that a noun was the best 'fit' in the places occupied by the nonsense words 'grindler', 'jandamest', and so on? Looking at its position within the sentence you can see that 'grindler' is preceded by 'a' and immediately followed by 'who': these clues point to a singular person (like a judge or prince). The ending of the word '-ler' is also found in other such nouns (e.g. babbler, swindler, wrestler). The word 'jandamest' is immediately preceded by the words 'in his' and followed by a full stop; these clues point to a noun of some sort. In addition, neither word ends in 's', another strong indication that they are singular. By contrast, 'esterflops' is preceded by the plural form of the verb ('were') and followed a little later on by a reference to 'these' – just two of the clues that point to a plural noun. A further clue is the ending of the word in 's', suggesting that there is a singular form 'esterflop'. And 'trepangle' is immediately preceded by 'the', a clear indication of a noun. Similar observations could be made about the remaining nouns.

All word classes can be subdivided into a number of smaller categories, though linguists often disagree over the details. As far as nouns are concerned, there are some subdivisions which are very useful when it comes to understanding how texts are constructed. Firstly, nouns can be broadly divided into **proper** and **common**. Proper nouns name particular identifiable persons, places and things, such as the person *Julius Caesar*, the city of *Rome*, the *White House* (the official residence of the US president), or the novel *Wuthering Heights*. Their special identity is emphasised by the use of capital letters. By contrast, common nouns name persons, places and things generally, such as an emperor, a city, a house or a novel.

Common nouns can be subdivided into **count** nouns and **mass** (or **non-count**) nouns. Count nouns refer to separate persons, places and things that can be counted (e.g. *goblins, castles* and *swords*). Mass nouns can't be counted (e.g. *fun, applause* and *laughter*). One further subdivision that applies to both count and mass nouns is that between **concrete** and **abstract**. Concrete nouns refer to anything that can be sensed physically such as *books, soldiers, butter, jewellery*; abstract nouns refer to things of the mind or the imagination such as *idea, love, knowledge, progress, luck*. Writers often make careful choices between these types of noun in order to achieve particular effects. As usual, however, you should note that these distinctions aren't always absolutely clear-cut. Some words, for example, can function as both mass and count nouns, depending on the context (e.g. *cheese/cheeses* or *grass/grasses*, where the second form can mean 'kinds of').

We've already spent some time examining the verb, since we first introduced it on page 9 as the part of the sentence that expresses an action, a process, or a state of existence. But again this definition is essentially semantic, and by itself is just too vague and unreliable. So let's look at the structural aspect. First of all, we know to expect at least one verb in every sentence. In the first sentence the word 'stompled' is immediately preceded by 'who', which here seems to be a relative pronoun introducing a relative clause (see page 36). The two groups of words 'from grilt to glot' and 'in his jandamest' appear to be adverbials, supplying information about how, when or where something was done. The only word unaccounted for is 'stompled', which additionally ends in '-ed' (as do 'frimped' and 'maldicated') as if to indicate past tense. We also know that the verb often occurs not as a single word but as a verb group (page 16). When we see the words 'would' and 'had to be', we know that another element in the verb group will almost certainly follow in order to complete the verb's meaning. The fact that 'he' immediately precedes 'frimped' further suggests that 'frimped' is also a verb.

The **adjective** typically is a word that modifies a noun, in other words it adds some description to it such as size (*large*), colour (*purple*), shape (*triangular*), or some other attribute or impression (*ancient* or *grotesque*). It normally precedes the noun that it's modifying, so if we've identified 'grindler' and 'arples' as nouns, it's most likely that 'prampsy' and 'vardy' are adjectives. Their ending in 'y' is also common among adjectives (e.g. *flimsy, hardy, nasty*). And if we examine 'prampsier', we see another common feature of adjectives, the manner in which they change their ending to '-er' to indicate a comparison between two things. By contrast, 'ulpsome' is part of the complement 'very ulpsome' following the copular verb 'was'. We can't be quite sure what might follow 'He was', but the next word 'very' provides the clue we need. The word 'very' can't normally be followed by a noun (e.g. He was very judge.), but can be followed by a large number of adjectives (e.g. *wise, large, old*). In addition, many adjectives end in '-some' (e.g. *gruesome, handsome, meddlesome*).

As with the term adjective, the term **adverb** is new, but in this case we've already discussed some important functions that it performs. Essentially, the adverb is a one-word adverbial. It describes how, when or where something is done, and as we've seen (page 30) its position in the sentence is more flexible. However, many adverbs typically occur next to or near the verb they modify, and many also end in '-ly'. Hence 'gloopsily' and 'armestically' seem to describe how the subject would 'frimp'. And just as, for instance, the adverbs *glossily* and *artistically* are formed from (or **derive** from) the adjectives *glossy* and *artistic*, so we could be fairly sure that 'gloopsily' and 'armestically' derive from the adjectives 'gloopsy' and 'armestic'.

This has been a lengthy and fairly detailed commentary, but it's indicative of the level of analysis necessary, if you're to use the information effectively. It should, of course, have reflected much of the discussion that took place during the Activity! Now return to page 51 for a summary of these findings.

COMMENTARY

On Activity 30

The general observation you should have made is that by themselves these words have little clear meaning. In fact, it's very hard to define or explain most of them. What, for instance, does 'a' mean? Or 'the'? Or 'but' and 'till'; 'he' and 'these'; 'was' and 'had'? Yet without these words each sentence collapses. These apparently insignificant words actually perform the vital function of holding the various bits of meaning together within a framework. They have minimal meaning in themselves; their key function is grammatical. So for instance, 'a' and 'the' primarily signal that a noun is coming up; 'but' and 'till' link the bits of meaning that precede and follow them; 'he' and 'these' refer to persons or things already identified; 'was' as a copular verb acts as a link and indicates tense; and 'had' also indicates tense. In contrast to content words, these are **function words**; their role is structural, and they also quite clearly show that Text 19 is essentially English, despite the many nonsense words included. The content words may be the essential bricks in constructing a text, but without the mortar of the function words there is nothing to hold the text together.

COMMENTARY

On Activity 31

The words in nadsat mean the following:

ittied = went; grahzny = dirty; devotchkas = young girls; veck = guy; nagoy = naked; von = stink; starry = ancient; domy = house; viddy = see; moloko = milk; kots = (male) cats; koshkas = (female) cats; scoteenas = beasts; malenky = little; crasted = stole; noga = foot or leg; rookers = hands; govoreet = talk.

Thus the word classes are:

Nouns:	devotchkas; veck; von; domy; moloko; kots; koshkas; scoteenas; devotchka; noga; rookers; govoreet.
Verbs:	ittied; viddy; crasted.
Adjectives:	grahzny; nagoy; starry; malenky.
P.S.	and droog = friend or mate!

COMMENTARY
On Activity 32

It's unlikely that anyone produced a grammatically unacceptable sequence of words, and if they did it was no doubt challenged strongly! Clearly some words are mutually exclusive (e.g. 'red' and 'blue', 'new' and 'old') because of their basic meanings. Likewise some function words can't occur together (e.g. 'a', 'the', 'my' and 'her'), but some can, though not consecutively ('quite' and 'very'). For instance, you can say 'quite old very pale red' but not 'quite very old' or 'very quite pale'.

Though the possible variations are potentially extremely varied, you should nevertheless have found that certain restrictions operate at each end of the description. The function words 'a', 'the', 'my' and 'her', if used, must normally come first, though exceptionally 'quite' can precede 'a' or 'the'. At the far end, you should have found that 'cotton', 'silk' or 'leather' immediately preceded 'hat' and that no other word could be inserted between them. Somewhere in the middle, you should have found that evaluative words like 'splendid' and 'brilliant' normally occur before any reference to the colour. In addition, some words have their own individual rules for combination, e.g. 'one'. Plainly the rules for description are complicated, and they can't be fully explored here. Nevertheless, it's clear yet again that you already possess a thorough knowledge of these rules, which you're able to follow both accurately and unconsciously.

COMMENTARY
On Activity 34

Everything occurring before the verb ('is' and 'has been criticized' respectively) is the subject. In contrast to the subsequent short verb phrases, these subjects are composed of quite lengthy and complicated noun phrases. Admittedly, both sentences have been taken out of context, but this doesn't alter the fact that the lengthy subjects put great demands on the reader. Why? Well, if you refer to our earlier discussion of the Given/New Contract (page 42), it becomes clear that the relative balance is uneven. In Text 22, all the information in the subject is new. In Text 23, the information isn't new, but is nevertheless quite complex and clearly summarises some difficult concepts. This loading of information into the subject is common in certain types of text, for example in promotional and advertising literature or in legal statutes. Of course, you can keep re-reading the sentence until you've fully grasped it, but there's often a case for rewriting the sentence in the interests of being reader-friendly.

Here are two suggested revised versions:

TEXT 22a

Tambourine Mountain, 560 metres above sea level, is a volcanic plateau with a maximum length of eight kilometres, a width of five kilometres, and just thirty kilometres inland from Queensland's Gold Coast.

TEXT 23a

David Lane has criticized the view of the USSR as a totalitarian society dominated by a ruling elite with absolute power, concerned primarily with furthering its own interests at the expense of the mass of the population.

The new versions aren't perfect, but they suggest that further thought might be given to rewriting the surrounding text as well. However, this 'front loading' of information into the subject can be an effective device in some contexts, as we'll see.

These subjects are remarkably diverse in length and type. A head has been italicised within each subject, but in some cases there's more than one. Some explanation is clearly needed! Let's identify the subjects of the sentences first:

1 India's most wanted Bandit *King*
2 Notorious *dacoit, cop-killer* and elephant *poacher Veerappan*, who sports a menacing handlebar moustache,
3 The *outlaw*, a dead *ringer* for Bollywood's biggest, baddest villain Gabbar Singh of Sholay fame,
4 The real-life *drama*
5 *Veerappan*, dressed in his distinctive combat gear,
6 the 72-year-old *superstar*
7 The *leading man*, with four decades in the movies and 220 films to his name,
8 The *hostage-takers* and their prize *catch*

Leaving aside the direct speech at the end of paragraph 6, the subjects at the beginning of these eight paragraphs refer four times to the bandit, twice to the victim, once to both (sentence 8) and once to the incident as a whole (sentence 4). The emphasis, foreshadowed in the headline and the subsequent bullet points, is clearly on the perpetrator of the kidnapping rather than on the victim. Sentence 8 is the only sentence with two separate subjects. They are linked by a coordinator so that the reader remains aware of both the criminals and the victim, but note that it's the criminals who are given prominence by being mentioned first. The heads in the noun phrases are variously at the beginning, middle or end, and so there are correspondingly different amounts of pre- and postmodification.

Premodification varies in complexity. Sentence 3 certainly deserves closer inspection. Here 'a dead ringer' is a second noun phrase, following 'The outlaw'. These two consecutive phrases refer to the same person, but each supplies a different piece of information. Rather than premodify one head extensively, writers often repeat a reference to the head of a noun phrase with another head. You get two for the price of one, so to speak. The second noun phrase runs alongside the first and technically is said to be **in apposition** to it. With this in mind we can now better understand the complexity of sentence 2. Here, three separate heads ('dacoit', 'cop-killer', 'poacher') stress three roles that, according to the article, Veerappan acts out in his life. Usually only two noun phrases occur in apposition, but here there are effectively four crammed together. Such front-loading of information is typical of journalistic prose. Note that noun phrases can be in apposition whatever their function. In sentence 1, for example, the object comprises two noun phrases in apposition: 'the legendary south Indian actor' and 'Rajkumar'.

The types of postmodification also vary: a finite relative clause in sentence 2 ('*who* sports a menacing handlebar moustache'), a non-finite clause in sentence 5 ('*dressed* in his distinctive combat gear'), a prepositional phrase in sentence 7 ('*with* four decades in the movies and 220 films to his name'). What is unusual about the various subjects is the amount and variety of information and description they contain. Many of the facts have little relevance to the actual kidnapping. There is an almost indiscriminate piling up of information – virtually a potted biography – that threatens to overwhelm the reader's processing capacity. Of course, much of this information won't be new to all readers, and some of it is already mentioned in the previous bullet points. The journalist uses this front-loading technique to remind readers of facts that he wishes to emphasise. Nevertheless, he has deliberately provided an unusually large amount of information in the grammatical subjects, so as to capture quickly the attention of readers and satisfy their curiosity. The highly concentrated grammatical structures complement the intensified emotive vocabulary. The grammar makes a fundamental contribution to the meaning.

COMMENTARY
On Activity 37

This was admittedly a taxing task, though one for which this book has prepared you for thinking about. There's no easy answer to it, and in this commentary we can only attend briefly to one or two aspects. Chomsky believed that we intuitively recognise certain grammatical structures, regardless of any meaning they might contain. When first confronted by this particular sentence, most people see it as possessing a recognisable pattern or *form* of words, and if they're asked to analyse it by word class, they generally offer the following:

	Adj	Adj	Noun	Verb	Adv
gg	Colorless	green	ideas	sleep	furiously.

You may also have come to this conclusion. On this assumption you could go on to argue that the first three words make up a noun phrase that *functions* as the subject, and that the fourth and fifth words *function* as the verb phrase. And many eminent people would agree with you. But all of this rests on your initial assumption about word classes.

Plainly the sentence is too contradictory and nonsensical to have any identifiable meaning, though this doesn't stop many people trying to wrench some sort of meaning from it! But if it has no meaning, how can we know that 'green' is an adjective? Why shouldn't it equally be a noun? Or a verb? And why shouldn't 'sleep' be a noun also? How can we really know what class of word each belongs to here if they don't convey any meaning as a group of words? The difference between a sentence and a random string of words is that a sentence communicates meaning. That's how we recognise it, whether it's a major sentence or a minor one.

But don't worry about which view might be correct. The most important thing is to have thought about and discussed the issue. It's simply another way of examining the crucial interrelationship between grammar and meaning.

Summary

In this chapter you have:

- learned to classify words by their various functions
- analysed the noun phrase category
- practised some of the different grammatical patterns possible in writing
- re-examined the interrelationship between grammar and meaning.

5 A Touch of the Verbals

In this chapter you will:

- explore the difference between the active and passive voice
- distinguish between transitive and intransitive verbs
- examine the wide range of meaning in auxiliary verbs.

First among many

This chapter concentrates upon the verb, by far the most important word in the sentence. You can gain some idea of its pre-eminent position when you realise that the words 'verb' and 'word' are historically closely connected. Our word 'verb' comes from the Latin 'verbum', which the Romans (those Romans again!) had first used to refer to any class of word, and only later to the verb in particular. The verb was the word! In fact, the Old English 'word' and the Latin 'verbum' both derive from a single form 'werdh', used by the remote ancestors of the Anglo-Saxons and the Romans to refer to any word. We still retain this more general sense when we speak of someone 'verbalising' (i.e. expressing in words) their feelings, or making a 'verbal agreement' (i.e. an agreement through spoken words). Only in the study of grammar does 'verbal' refer specifically to verbs.

Do as you would be done by

The first verbal aspect we'll consider is the distinction between what is referred to as the **active voice** and the **passive voice**. Although these two terms refer to alternative ways of arranging the components of a clause or sentence, it's the verb that's the key to distinguishing between them. You can write many sentences in either form, so let's examine a typical pair:

a The emu pecked the interviewer.
b The interviewer was pecked by the emu.

The meaning of the two sentences is essentially the same, yet each conveys a difference in emphasis. In **a** the emphasis is on the emu that did the pecking, but in **b** the emphasis is on the person who was pecked. How is this achieved? Well, let's first apply the two-stage method for identifying the subject (page 18). So, in **a** the verb is 'pecked', and the answer to 'Who or what pecked?' is 'The emu'. In **b** the verb group is 'was pecked', and the answer to 'Who or what was pecked?' is 'The interviewer'. The change of subject initially attracts our attention to a different aspect of the sentence. Sentence **a** is about the emu; sentence **b** is about the interviewer. We could also say, in the absence of any contradictory evidence, that the subject in each sentence represents the Given information, while the verb phrase represents the New (see page 42). To account further for this change in emphasis, let's take a closer look at the two subjects.

The emu in **a** is the active participant in the sentence; it's the doer or performer of the action and is known technically as the **agent**. The verb 'pecked' is said to be active because it describes the action that the subject performs. If we look at **b**, we can see that the interviewer takes no action. The verb group 'was pecked' is said to be passive because the subject, the interviewer, is now the passive participant who is affected by the action described in the verb. He himself is doing nothing, but he's certainly having something done to him! Of course, 'the emu' in **b** is still the agent (because it's still doing the pecking), but as it isn't the subject it no longer appears a central part of the sentence. Notice also how you can further increase the emphasis on the interviewer in **b** by omitting the last three words 'by the emu', so removing all mention of the agent.

At first sight, then, it may have appeared unnecessary to have two different constructions to express the same meaning, but on closer inspection we can see that the choice of grammatical structure has a direct effect on the meaning. Nevertheless, the passive voice is less common than the active, and requires a more complicated verb group. There's also some evidence from psychological research that people on average take slightly longer to understand the passive form. Children before age seven generally aren't proficient in understanding or using it. But let's see the passive in action!

The Illustrated Police News was a highly popular Victorian weekly paper that reported crimes and disasters in a sensationalised and melodramatic fashion, accompanied by imaginative rather than accurate engravings. The account on the following page comes from the edition of 15 July 1871.

ACTIVITY 38

1 In pairs, examine Text 25 on the following page and mark every occurrence of a verb in the passive form. Why do you think the writer chose to use the passive voice instead of the active voice?

2 In pairs, rewrite the text by changing all the passive constructions into active ones. Remember that you'll need to change both the form of the verb and its subject; however, you should aim to retain as much of the original wording as possible. This is not quite

as easy as it may seem! What is the effect of the changes?

3 In larger groups or as a class, first agree upon all the examples of passive verbs. Then discuss the problems you've experienced in rewriting the passage, and the reasons for them. You should also discuss the contrasting effects wherever you were successful in writing an alternative version.

Now read the commentary on this Activity at the end of the chapter.

TEXT 25

Shocking Murder at a Bank
(15 / 7 / 1871)

The cashier of the Northern Bank at Newton Stewart, County Tyrone, Ireland, has been murdered, and the bank robbed of its cash, the unfortunate man having been discovered shortly after four o'clock on Thursday afternoon, lying beside the open safe where the cash was kept, his skull having been beaten in, and a box which should have contained £1,600 lying empty beside him.

No trace has yet been discovered which can lead to the detection of the murderer, but every effort is being made to find him out.

Further details of this atrocious murder have now come to hand, from which it appears that a customer was in the Bank transacting business at about three o'clock in the afternoon, and was the last person except the murderer who saw Mr Glass alive.

The murder was not discovered until a quarter past four o'clock, when a servant-maid in the bank came downstairs to see the time through the office door, and when looking in she saw a quantity of blood on the floor and becoming frightened ran out for a neighbour who returned with her. The two opened the door and proceeding to the office found the body extended on the floor, outside the counter. The face was turned downward with the feet toward the door. The mutilation caused to the head was horrible in the extreme, and displayed the utmost possible brutality. From the appearance of the wounds they had all been struck from behind, suddenly and unawares. Strange to say, though all the notes were taken out of the cash box, a quantity of gold was left behind.

Although we remarked earlier that young children demonstrate some lack of competence with the passive voice, it nevertheless appears quite frequently in books aimed at the older primary school child. Overleaf is a short extract from a simple introductory book on natural disasters called *Landslides and Avalanches* by Terry Jennings.

TEXT 26

[1]Every year about 100 million people go on holiday to the European Alps. [2]About 150 of them are killed by avalanches. [3]In the United States nearly 500 people have been killed by avalanches since 1950. [4]Wherever there are mountains there is a risk that avalanches will occur.

[5]There is little chance of surviving an avalanche. [6]Many people are killed instantly by the force of the avalanche. [7]About 70 per cent of victims do not survive longer than 20 minutes in the freezing conditions. [8]Trained dogs are used to search for avalanche victims. [9]It takes a dog half an hour to search an area that it would take 20 people four hours to cover.

ACTIVITY 39

1 In pairs, identify in Text 26 the sentences containing passive forms and sentences containing dummy subjects (page 42). What is the combined effect of these grammatical structures?

2 Still in pairs, rewrite the passage, using only active sentences and avoiding the use of a dummy subject. If you wish, you can combine some sentences.

3 Exchange your rewritten version with that of another pair and compare them. What differences in emphasis are there between these and the original? Why did the author choose to write it the way he did?

ACTIVITY 40

1 Individually, over say a week, search for other texts that make a significant use of the passive voice, and identify the reasons for this. (You might for instance look at textbooks describing scientific research or experiment, at broadsheet newspaper reports of political debates, or any fairly formal document issued by central or local government.) Bring these texts into class for comparison and discussion.

2 To complement this, again over a week, individually find a short passage written in the active voice, either fiction or non-fiction, and try to convert it into the passive. Did you find any clauses that you couldn't convert? Bring your text into class for a discussion of your relative success and any problems you experienced.

3 As an alternative to **2** above, turn to Text 12 on page 26 and in pairs rewrite it in the passive. What effect does this have on the description? Which three clauses can't be transformed into the passive? Why not?

4 In groups, compare your versions and discuss the resulting effect.

Who (or what) is Sylvia?

Before we examine another important feature of verbs (called transitivity), we need to expand on our discussion of the direct object. So far, we've seen that the direct object answers the question 'Did who or what?' in relation to a verb (page 22), and that it's generally a noun phrase (page 53). So, in

c   Bruno wrote a letter.

it's plain that 'a letter' is a noun phrase functioning as a direct object in answer to the question 'wrote what?' Fine. But in

d   Bruno wrote Sylvia a letter.

we seem at first sight to have a problem. What, grammatically, is Sylvia? It may *look* like a direct object because it's a noun phrase (consisting of one proper noun) and it does follow the verb. But it doesn't answer our earlier test question 'wrote what?' As far as we can tell, Bruno didn't write *the word* 'Sylvia' somewhere! And 'a letter' can't be in apposition (page 68) to 'Sylvia', as the two noun phrases refer to completely different things. An alternative version of **d** reveals the answer:

e   Bruno wrote a letter to Sylvia.

It's obvious that 'a letter' remains the direct object, and that Bruno wrote not 'Sylvia' but 'to Sylvia'. We're once again dealing with ellipsis (page 9). Sentence **d** is an elliptical version of **e** in that 'to' has been omitted from what was in its full version a prepositional phrase 'to Sylvia' (page 57). 'Sylvia' isn't the direct object of the verb 'wrote', even though it's a noun phrase in **d**. Instead, it's called the **indirect object**, on the basis that the person (in this case 'Sylvia') is, so to speak, 'at one remove' from the direct action expressed in the verb. In other words, what Bruno actually did was to write the letter, but this wasn't simply an end in itself. We assume that he wrote it with the intention of sending it *to* Sylvia.

Some points to note:

- the relationship between the verb and its two objects is clearly different: the action of the verb directly affects only the direct object (hence its name)
- the direct object comes *after* the indirect object when the latter is a noun phrase, as in **d**, but comes *before* the indirect object when this is a prepositional phrase, as in **e**
- where the indirect object is a noun phrase, the direct object can't normally be omitted (e.g. 'Bruno wrote Sylvia' is incomplete; it requires the mention of what Bruno wrote).

Who (or what) is cooking?

Many common verbs can be followed by both a direct and an indirect object, e.g. *bring, buy, cook, feed, find, give, lend, offer, save, write*. Very often their direct object is a thing, while their indirect object is a person with the preposition 'to' or 'for' implied. For example, compare

f   Sylvia cooked Bruno a pumpkin.

in which the indirect object 'Bruno' is followed by the direct object 'a pumpkin', with

g   Sylvia cooked a pumpkin for Bruno.

in which the direct object 'a pumpkin' is followed by the indirect object 'Bruno'. The meaning of both sentences is *essentially* the same, though the following Activity will help you modify this basic statement.

1 In pairs, choose five of the verbs listed in the previous paragraph and create pairs of sentences with the same meaning, using **f** and **g** as models.

2 Note whether the preposition attached to the indirect object is 'to' or 'for'. Can any verbs take either preposition and, if so, does the meaning alter?

3 In larger groups, compare your findings.

Though your pairs of sentences have essentially the same meaning, do you detect any difference in emphasis, depending on the order of the two objects?

Now read the detailed commentary on this Activity at the end of the chapter before you read on.

A hot touch of the verbals

Here's an extract from the final two pages of *Hot Touch*, a romance by Deborah Smith.

TEXT 27

Caroline laughed softly. 'Wonderful.'

'Talking to some animal I don't see?' Paul teased. He put his arm around her and drew her to him.

Caroline looked up into his face and didn't speak for a moment, enjoying the rush of pleasure she felt when she lost herself in his eyes.

'Thank you for indulging my need to walk,' she whispered. They'd left the Corvette near the end of the driveway.

Paul caressed her face tenderly. 'It's been a long, strange day. The walk feels good.' He cupped her chin in one hand and studied her face. 'How are you, *chère*? The truth.'

'Better,' she said in a thoughtful tone. 'Much better than I've ever been in my life. And peaceful.'

'*Bien.*' Stepping back, he took her hands in his and looked at her with a quiet intensity that sent tingles up her spine. 'Mademoiselle Caroline, will you marry a Cajun veterinarian who doesn't care about being rich or living fancy but who'll love you like no other man on the face of the earth?'

Caroline squinted at the trees overhead as if thinking. 'I believe I'm as smart as my mother,' she said finally. 'I know what's important.' She looked at Paul so raptly that he began to smile.

'Say it,' he whispered.

She brought his hands to her lips. 'I'll marry you,' she answered, kissing them. 'You're my lifemate and I'll never want anyone else.'

They stood in the driveway a long time, just holding each other. Long golden shadows slanted through the oaks when she and Paul finally walked into the yard, savoring every moment of a glorious fall sunset.

A fairly commonplace passage, you'd say, portraying a stereotypical couple who from the outset were pretty obviously destined to spend an idyllic life together. Perhaps, but how exactly does the writing convey this? Partly through the choice of highly conventional vocabulary (e.g. 'tingles up her spine', 'lifemate', and the final description of the sunset); partly through the switches between the characters' dialogue and the author's description and comment on the scene; but partly – and this is our concern – through the grammar.

1 In small groups, draw up a table of all the verbs used to describe the interaction between the two characters (you should ignore the actual dialogue between them). Identify whether the verbs are associated with the male or the female character, and whether or not they are followed by a direct object.

2 In larger groups or as a class, compare your analysis and reach agreement. Discuss in what ways the verbs associated with the two characters differ. How do these differences reinforce the stereotypical portrayal of the characters?

You should read the commentary on this Activity at the end of the chapter before reading on.

Ruby – an icon for crossing?

The commentary to the above Activity has shown that the choice of verbs and direct objects, and the resulting grammatical patterns or colligations (see page 41), contribute significantly to the meaning of a text. We now need to examine more systematically the options available. Let's take a look at some examples, beginning with

h   Ruby painted an icon.

You'll immediately recognise this as a simple sentence of the SVO kind, the finite verb 'painted' taking the noun phrase 'an icon' as its direct object. Any verb that takes a direct object is said to be **transitive**, a word which simply means 'going across'. In other words, the meaning of the verb is expanded by going across to the person or thing directly affected by it. However, we can choose to omit the direct object:

i   Ruby painted.

The sentence is now less informative but still perfectly acceptable grammatically. The verb 'painted' is still said to be transitive, because it *implies* a direct object of some kind as yet unstated but that could be added (e.g. 'a portrait', 'a geranium', 'her garden gate'). Fine, but what about

j   Ruby found an icon.

Structurally this looks exactly like **h**, but if we delete the direct object we get

k   Ruby found.

which is distinctly odd and certainly isn't grammatically acceptable. Here you haven't the option to omit the direct object; you *must* complete the meaning by providing one. Now let's examine

l   Ruby snored.

This seems structurally like **i** in that it makes perfect sense and is grammatically acceptable without a direct object. And yet … we *can't* add a direct object! We can of course add a number of adverbials that inform us how, when, and where Ruby snored, as in

m   Ruby snored tunefully late at night in her hammock.

but the questions 'Snored who or what?' or 'What did Ruby snore?' have no meaning. The verb 'to snore' doesn't take a direct object. Accordingly, it's said to be **intransitive**.

In summary, then, we have three types of verb:

- transitive verbs with the *option* of taking a direct object (e.g. 'paint')
- transitive verbs that must take a direct object (e.g. 'find')
- intransitive verbs that can't take a direct object (e.g. 'snore').

Before we explore another passage, let's examine some typical verbs:

read, forget, queue, hit, disappear, complain, take, dress, die, arrange, kick, smell, destroy, ring.

ACTIVITY 43

1 In pairs, decide which of the above verbs are transitive (i.e. either must or optionally can take a direct object) and which intransitive (i.e. can't take a direct object). The simplest method of discovering this is by creating short sentences using the verbs, but be sure you're adding only a noun phrase and that this represents a *direct*, not an indirect, object! (see page 74)

2 Now look at your list of transitive verbs and subdivide them into those that must take a direct object and those that don't have to.

3 In larger groups compare your findings. Can the meaning change significantly for any verbs that you categorised as optionally taking a direct object?

Now read the commentary on this Activity at the end of the chapter before continuing here.

If you return to Text 27 you'll now appreciate that the contrast in characterisation, as described in the commentary to Activity 42, is achieved in great part by using verbs either transitively or intransitively. Conventional romantic fiction has perpetuated the stereotypical images of the dominant aggressive male and the submissive emotional female. More recently, however, much writing has in varying degrees attempted to reverse these traditional roles.

ACTIVITY 44

1 Individually, rewrite Text 27 by ensuring that Paul is associated with verbs used intransitively and Caroline with verbs used transitively. You should also choose verbs signifying action or movement for Caroline and verbs signifying mental processes and emotional states for Paul. Alternatively, follow these guidelines but create your own setting and characters.

2 In small groups, share your rewritten versions and discuss how successfully they have reversed the traditional roles of male and female. To what extent did the choice of verb contribute to the overall effect?

3 As an alternative and longer-term individual investigation, find two or three examples of fiction from one genre (e.g. romantic, detective, sci-fi, or horror) in which contrasting uses of verbs (transitive and intransitive, active and passive, or both) reflect the difference in relationship between two characters. You should choose a key scene from each source and analyse the ways in which the verbs are used. Write up your findings and discussion of the significant contrasts between your texts.

Can't make the transition!

And finally on the topic of transitivity, the following Text is from *The Inheritors* by William Golding. It's set in prehistoric times and tells the story of a small tribe of primitive Neanderthals who encounter a more advanced species of human. This extract describes a conflict between Lok, a Neanderthal who has been watching the new species from a treetop, and a member of these newcomers (the 'other') who from across a river attacks Lok with a bow and arrow.

TEXT 28

The bushes twitched again. Lok steadied by the tree and gazed. A head and a chest faced him, half-hidden. There were white bone things behind the leaves and hair. The man had white bone things above his eyes and under the mouth so that his face was longer than a face should be. The man turned sideways in the bushes and looked at Lok along his shoulder. A stick rose upright and there was a lump of bone in the middle. Lok peered at the stick and the lump of bone and the small eyes in the bone things over the face. Suddenly Lok understood that the man was holding the stick out to him but neither he nor Lok could reach across the river. He would have laughed if it were not for the echo of the screaming in his head. The stick began to grow shorter at both ends. Then, it shot out to full length again.

The dead tree by Lok's ear acquired a voice.

'Clop!'

His ears twitched and he turned to the tree. By his face there had grown a twig: a twig that smelt of other, and of goose, and of the bitter berries that Lok's stomach told him he must not eat. This twig had a white bone at the end. There were hooks in the bone and sticky brown stuff hung in the crooks. His nose examined this stuff and did not like it. He smelled along the shaft of the twig. The leaves on the twig were red feathers and reminded him of goose. He was lost in a generalized astonishment and excitement.

ACTIVITY 45

1 In small groups, make a list of all the verbs used transitively and all those used intransitively, together with a note of the grammatical subjects that they relate to.
2 In larger groups or as a class, compare your findings and reach agreement. What is unusual about some of the subjects to the verbs? How many verbs associated with Lok are used transitively and how many intransitively? What is the overall effect of the verbs used intransitively?

There is a commentary on this Activity at the end of the chapter.

The numbers game?

In Chapter 4 (page 52) we noted that auxiliary verbs are frequently added to the main verb within the verb group in order to provide further information of various kinds. So far we've looked at the way some auxiliaries indicate tense, person and number. These so-called **primary auxiliaries** actually represent specialised uses of the verbs 'to be', 'to have' and 'to do', all three of which also function independently as main verbs. In other words, they can convey complete meaning without relying upon another verb, as in

n Sylvia *is* a fantastic cook.

o Bruno *has* an insatiable appetite for pumpkin.

p Sylvia and Bruno *do* the dishes together every night.

If we compare **n** and **o** to

q Sylvia is *marrying* a fantastic cook.

r Bruno has *conquered* an insatiable appetite for pumpkin.

in both of which the main verb is italicised, we can see that the remaining verb in each verb group ('is' and 'has') is now relegated to the position of an auxiliary. Naturally, the meaning has fundamentally changed. The auxiliary 'do' is more complex, but it's often called upon to indicate tense when transforming declaratives into interrogatives, as for example where the present tense

s Ruby loves Bruno.

becomes

t *Does* Ruby love Bruno?

or where the past tense

u Bruno loved Ruby.

becomes

v *Did* Bruno love Ruby?

But there's a small number of other auxiliaries that perform a quite critical task, even though they can't normally occur without another main verb. Let's first take a look at an extract from *Numerology – Your Love and Relationship Guide*, a book that explores the allegedly magical influence of numbers in people's lives, by Sonia Ducie.

TEXT 29

Family life is a natural part of your life as you love to relate to those who you are closest to. You may well have been brought up in a loving and caring home where you were nurtured and looked after, or it could be that you were called upon to do the caring for your family. Whenever there were problems you may have been the one to listen, or were you a little monkey and played your sister off against your brother, or mother against your father and got up to mischief? Perhaps you were the middle child, so that you could feel what it was like to have two other siblings to choose from, and maybe you didn't like playing piggy in the middle at all.

With the influence of the 2 you may dislike being in the middle of any situation where you need to take sides, particularly at home. This may be between your parents, or between your wife or husband and your children (such as in situations of divorce). You can be pretty uncompromising sometimes when you are put on the spot, and you may manipulate situations or people to avoid making direct decisions at times. However, you are open-hearted and, particularly with a divorce, you may well like to see both sides win and to come to some sort of amicable agreement. Indeed, divorce is one of the most painful facts of life; with a 2 it can seem unbearably painful because of the depth of your emotions.

ACTIVITY 46

1 In small groups, examine Text 29 and identify all the words and phrases that indicate a lack of certainty and definiteness. Which words in particular do you find recurring?

2 In larger groups or as a class, compare your findings and then discuss the likely reasons for the vagueness and uncertainty within the text. How do they reflect the target audience for the text?

Now read the commentary at the end of the chapter before reading on.

Verbs with attitude!

It's the weekend. 'Are you going to finish that essay before you come out with us?' you're asked. You reply: 'No, I would finish it but ... well, I could finish it ... I might ... er, I should finish it, I suppose ... I can finish it ... I must ... yes, I *will* finish it.' As you turn the question over in your mind, your attitude undergoes a number of changes from serious doubt (*would*) through increasing degrees of possibility (*could* and *might*) to a feeling of personal obligation (*should*) to acknowledgement of your ability (*can*) to necessity (*must*) and finally to a firm intention (*will*). These changes in attitude are conveyed by a number of auxiliary verbs, each of which adds something extra to the basic statement about finishing the essay. And what they add is **modality**: the attitude of the speaker or writer to whatever they are saying or writing. They are properly termed **modal auxiliaries**, in other words auxiliaries that indicate modality, and the most common and important ones are:

can	may	shall	will	must
could	might	should	would	ought to

These modal auxiliaries are necessarily tied to main verbs because they add attitude to the basic meaning. There is no independent verb such as 'to may', 'to might' or 'to must'. And what are the attitudes that can be conveyed? Well, the most frequent are those of possibility, probability, permission, ability, uncertainty, certainty, intention, necessity, obligation, and insistence. Of course, modality can also be expressed by other means. Text 29 included the words 'perhaps' and 'maybe'; others like 'possibly', 'conceivably', 'likely' and 'probably' often occur in texts. However, modal auxiliaries are immensely useful and powerful grammatical words that demonstrate yet again how grammar shapes meaning.

ACTIVITY 47

1 In pairs or small groups, rewrite Text 29 by removing all modal auxiliaries, and any other words and phrases indicating uncertainty. What are the difficulties in performing this task?

2 As a class, compare the difficulties you experienced and examine your rewritten versions. How successful are they in overcoming these difficulties?

1 In pairs, take the simple sentence 'Xavier and Xanthe make meringues', and add each of the ten modal auxiliaries in turn (e.g. 'Xavier and Xanthe can make meringues'). Decide what extra meaning is expressed in each case.

2 In larger groups, compare your findings.

What can you say about the meaning of each modal auxiliary?

Be sure to read the commentary to this Activity at the end of the chapter before reading on.

Child's play

The following two texts are from *The Parents' A to Z* by Penelope Leach. Text 30 is the opening of a section dealing with the storage of toys; Text 31 discusses the child's possible anxiety when starting school.

TEXT 30

Storage

Lack of storage space may limit, even more than lack of money, the playthings you can make available to your child. Poor storage can also make what she does have virtually unusable because she cannot see what is there or find all the bits of anything.

Unless you positively enjoy sorting out cupboards and drawers (probably weekly and certainly monthly) you may find that it is a mistake to try and store the toys of this age group in a way which banishes them from adult sight. A range of open shelves is often more efficient and it can look good, too, if trouble is taken.

You could, for example, accumulate five-litre plastic ice-cream containers and some plastic seed trays and use them for keeping all her small toys, or toys with many separate parts. Large, heavy toys and the ones to which she is allowed to help herself at any time, can go on the lowest shelves; things you want her to have to ask for, plus the ones she uses least, can go higher up. She can be reminded of what is there, even in the boxes she cannot reach, by having one item glued on the outside of the box or a picture of it drawn with felt-tip pen.

You may find that some playthings are best stored hanging up in bags. Drawstring bags are easy to make, either out of a pretty fabric or out of nylon 'string' so that she can see what is in them. Different sizes will take anything from a collection of balls to her favourite dressing-up clothes and accessories.

TEXT 31

Anxiety when starting school

Starting school is a very big step for most children and an enormous one for some. You should almost expect an upsurge of anxiety in your child because, however capable you have helped him to feel so far, he is almost certain to wonder whether he can cope without you in this new big group with its vast noisy buildings, countless children, many so much larger than he, and all these strange adults with apparently limitless authority and power (*see also* **School**/Starting school).

Steady (almost boring) home support and home routines will see most children through. But where there are real problems over going to school or fears of events within it, you must now work with the teacher because you do not have the actual power to influence what happens to him, minute by minute and day by day when you are not there. Remember that:

Fear creates fear so that even if he overcomes his anxiety and goes into school each morning, the fact that he does so *feeling anxious* is likely to make a vicious circle. If he feels sick and shaky every Monday morning, those horrible feelings will become linked in his mind with school and he will come to dread the feelings as much as the school. He may even go on having the anxiety-symptoms after he has actually come to enjoy the business of being at school. So, as before, the important consideration is that anxiety should be avoided if it possibly can be. Your aim is not just to get him there but to get him there feeling happy.

ACTIVITY 49

1 In small groups, examine Text 30 and Text 31 in turn. List all the modal auxiliaries and any other words or phrases that express modality. Identify the predominant modalities expressed (e.g. ability, possibility, certainty) in each text.

2 In larger groups or as a class, compare your findings. What are the predominant modalities in each text and how do they reflect the different purposes of each?

ACTIVITY 50

1 Individually, collect three different types of text that include a significant number of modal auxiliaries. (Political speeches and horoscopes are obvious examples, but there are many others.)

2 List the modal auxiliaries used in each and identify the main modalities (e.g. possibility, obligation, certainty) that are used. Why has

the writer in each case adopted a particular attitude towards the topic of the text and the target audience?

3 Later, in small groups, you should each present at least one of your texts and explain why it makes use of the particular modalities you have identified.

COMMENTARY

On Activity 38

The passive verb forms you should have identified are:

Sentence	Passive verb form
1	has been murdered; robbed; having been discovered; was kept; having been beaten in
2	has … been discovered; is being made
3	*none*
4	was not discovered
5	*none*
6	was turned
7	caused
8	had … been struck
9	were taken out; was left.

If you experienced any difficulty in identifying all the passive forms, notice that in every case the verb group must include the past participle (page 17) as its final part. So, for instance, in the first sentence 'has been *murdered*' is followed shortly afterwards by '*robbed*' (where the repetition of 'has been' is omitted – an example of ellipsis). Both past participles have been italicised.

The principal obstacle to rewriting the passage is that the agent or doer for some of the actions is not explicitly mentioned, e.g. in sentence 1: the person or persons who murdered, robbed and beat the cashier; the person who kept the cash; the person who discovered the man; or in sentence 2: the person or persons who haven't yet discovered a trace but are making every effort. The only agent explicitly mentioned anywhere is the 'servant-maid' who discovered the body. So in order to reconstruct the text you've to name the agents, e.g. 'An unknown assailant murdered ...' or 'The police have not yet discovered any trace ...' It may seem awkward and convoluted to use the passive, but it can have some distinct advantages:

- the writer can focus on the *results* of the actions, e.g. the victim, the crime
- the writer can avoid identifying the persons responsible, whether the assailant (because they are unknown) or the authorities (because of potential embarrassment)
- though agents are unnamed, the writer can rely upon the reader to infer their existence from the context
- the writer can convey a more formal and impersonal attitude to the events (e.g. to the fact that no one has discovered any trace).

COMMENTARY
On Activity 41

You should have had little difficulty in performing this task and distinguishing between the different meanings that the prepositions 'to' and 'for' give to the verbs *bring, feed, give, lend, offer*, and *write*. You should also have discovered that in some cases the version that omits a preposition could imply either. So

w   Sylvia brought Bruno a pumpkin.

could mean either that she brought one 'to' him or 'for' him. In other cases the version without the preposition implies only one. So

x   Sylvia offered Bruno a pumpkin.

can mean only that she offered a pumpkin 'to' him, not 'for' him. We clearly don't always have the option of using either version!

As to any difference in emphasis, you may well have felt this to be slightly stronger for the second object, whether direct or indirect. If you were undecided, that's fine! After all, it's virtually impossible to tell in most isolated sentences just where the emphasis lies. On the basis that most sentences move from Given to New information, the general tendency is for the emphasis to occur somewhere on the New. This merely reflects our expectations as readers or listeners, for in either case we're impatient to learn *more* (i.e. something New). Let's briefly revisit two earlier sentences:

f   Sylvia cooked Bruno a pumpkin.
g   Sylvia cooked a pumpkin for Bruno.

In **f** it's natural to feel a slightly greater emphasis on the final noun phrase 'a pumpkin', whereas in **g** it seems to occur on the final prepositional phrase 'for Bruno'. This phenomenon is termed **end focus**. And if we could see either of these two sentences as part of a larger text, such a feeling might well be confirmed. So for instance in

y   He was ravenous. Sylvia cooked Bruno a pumpkin.

clearly the emphasis is on the New information concerning what exactly Sylvia cooked. But in the following sentence:

z   All the men were ravenous. Sylvia cooked Bruno a pumpkin.

there's plainly a greater emphasis on the particular person that Sylvia chose to cook for. But for as long as **f** and **g** remain *isolated from any larger context*, we can't be sure.

Apart from context the other key factor that influences emphasis, in speech, is of course intonation, specifically stress. We can read **f** and stress any one of the five words to indicate what we consider to be the essential focus of the whole utterance. So:

aa   SYLVIA cooked Bruno a pumpkin. [not Vesta]
bb   Sylvia COOKED Bruno a pumpkin. [not sold]
cc   Sylvia cooked BRUNO a pumpkin. [not Tarquin]
dd   Sylvia cooked Bruno A pumpkin. [not several]
ee   Sylvia cooked Bruno a PUMPKIN. [not a marrow]

This ability to indicate focus by how we say something rather than by how we choose to order our words – by intonation as opposed to grammar – demonstrates the versatility of speech. It also allows us greater freedom of choice in grammatical matters when we speak, whereas in writing we have to exercise far greater care if we want to convey our meaning clearly and unambiguously. Here the way in which sentences are constructed and linked to one another is critical. We deal specifically with this matter of linking, or **cohesion**, in the next chapter.

Generally, our expectation may be that the focus of any sentence is on the later New information (i.e. end focus), but we must be aware that this certainly won't always be the case. Otherwise language would be too predictable and uninteresting. One way to indicate focus in a sentence is by bringing the specific element to the front in a separate clause. So, returning to our two cooks once more, in

f   Sylvia cooked Bruno a pumpkin.

we can focus unambiguously on Sylvia, Bruno or the pumpkin respectively by redrafting it as one of the following:

ff   It was *Sylvia* who cooked Bruno a pumpkin.
gg   It was *Bruno* that Sylvia cooked a pumpkin for.
hh   It was *a pumpkin* that Sylvia cooked for Bruno.

The separate clause at the beginning of each sentence, together with the change in expected word order, produce a strong focus on the complement following 'was'. This type of sentence is called a **cleft sentence**, because what would normally be a sentence of just one clause has been split into two clauses, each with its own verb. It's a fairly uncommon sentence type, but it's useful for establishing focus in writing, where intonation isn't possible.

What is again apparent from this admittedly lengthy commentary is that our choice of word order, in clauses and in sentences, affects significantly the meaning we are communicating.

If you carried out the initial task methodically, you should have listed the following verbs and direct objects:

Caroline		Paul	
Verb	**Direct object**	**Verb**	**Direct object**
laughed		teased	
looked		put	his arm
didn't speak		drew	her
enjoying	the rush of pleasure	caressed	her face
felt		cupped	her chin
lost	herself	studied	her face
whispered		took	her hands
said		looked	
squinted		sent	tingles
thinking		began to smile	
said		whispered	
looked			
brought	his hands		
answered			
kissing	them		

We can see some revealing differences in the verbs associated with each character. Let's summarise these. Firstly Paul:

■ most verbs indicate some action instigated by Paul that affects Caroline in some respect (e.g. 'drew', 'caressed')
■ most of the verbs describe physical movement (e.g. 'put', 'cupped', 'took')
■ the direct objects complete the action of the verbs by stating explicitly what has been affected (e.g. 'caressed her face').

Secondly Caroline:

■ a higher proportion of verbs have Caroline as their subject
■ several verbs indicate not actions but states of mind (e.g. 'enjoying', 'felt', 'thinking')
■ only four of the 15 verbs have direct objects, and only two of these are concerned with the completion of actions relating to Paul ('brought his hands' and 'kissing them').

The effect of this contrastive use of verbs and direct objects is to reinforce the male as the person in control, the person who takes action that directly affects the female. (This is further reinforced by the repeated use of 'her' as either a pronoun or possessive determiner – see pages 54–55). By contrast the female merely responds rather than takes the initiative. She is far more involved in her own mental processes and emotional states than in physical action; only two verbs are followed by an explicit direct object relating to something outside of her ('his hands' and 'them'). She is portrayed as the more sensitive and reflective of the two, and this portrayal is achieved in no small part by the grammatical choices of verbs and direct objects.

COMMENTARY

On Activity 43

You should have had little difficulty in classifying the verbs as follows:

Intransitive	Transitive only	Transitive (with optional direct object)
queue	hit	read
disappear	take	forget
complain	destroy	dress
die	arrange	kick
		smell
		ring

However, we might make a couple of further observations here. Firstly, although the verbs in the third column are transitive, when they are used *without* a direct object it's more accurate to describe them as *behaving intransitively*, because superficially they appear intransitive. In fact, you can say that all verbs behave transitively or intransitively. For example, 'die' is normally used intransitively because you simply don't add a direct object. Yet by now we've come to expect exceptions, and so exceptionally you can say 'He died a terrible death.' Here the verb 'die' is being used transitively, though 'death' is the only word that can occur as this particular verb's direct object.

Secondly, you should have detected a change of meaning in the uses of 'dress' and 'smell'. When used intransitively 'dress' implies an action relating back to the subject. For instance, in 'He dressed' we know that the reflexive pronoun (see page 55) 'himself' is implied, not any other object. Other verbs that behave like this include *undress, wash,* and *shave.* The change in meaning with 'smell' is more dramatic! Used transitively the verb refers to an action performed by the subject (e.g. 'He smells the flowers'); used intransitively it describes the state of the subject (e.g. 'That curry smells wonderful' or 'He smells').

COMMENTARY

On Activity 45

Several grammatical subjects in this passage have unusual verbs of action and movement attributed to them. These include parts of the body (e.g. 'A head and a chest *faced*', 'Lok's stomach *told*', 'His nose *examined*') and inanimate objects (e.g. 'A stick *rose*', 'The dead tree ... *acquired*'). Lok himself is generally the subject of a verb used intransitively (e.g. 'Lok *steadied* ... and *gazed*', '*laughed*', '*smelled*'). Additionally, most of these verbs indicate sensory perception (e.g. '*gazed*', '*peered*', '*smelled*') or basic mental processes (e.g. '*understood*') rather than physical action. The effect of these grammatical choices is to allow us an insight into Lok's undeveloped consciousness. As readers, we see and experience this scene through Lok's mind. The various inanimate grammatical subjects indicate that Lok doesn't understand the true cause of events. Not only does he fail to recognise that 'the stick' is actually a weapon, he is also unaware that it's the other man who's controlling it, firing a poisoned arrow at him with potentially lethal consequences. Ironically, the one thing Lok believes he understands – that the man is holding 'the stick' out to him – is a complete misunderstanding. Lok doesn't appreciate that actions produce effects, as the firing of the bow is described intransitively as 'it *shot out* to full length again', while the appearance of the arrow in the tree he perceives as a sudden natural growth. The cumulative effect of the intransitively used verbs associated with Lok, together with the subjects that function as agents without any recognition of human control, is to suggest a sense of Lok's confused and limited understanding of both himself and his environment. These grammatical features occur frequently within a small amount of text. We can therefore say that there are recurring patterns (or colligations) that contribute significantly to the meaning of this passage.

COMMENTARY
On Activity 46

You should have discovered a number of words and phrases that suggest a lack of certainty, e.g. *may well, it could be, Whenever, may have been, Perhaps, maybe, may dislike, This may be, You can be pretty uncompromising sometimes, may manipulate, may well like, some sort of, it can seem.* You may also think that the alternatives offered by the conjunction *or* suggest uncertainty. Particular words that recur are *may* (six times), *can* and *could* (twice each).

Why so much vagueness and uncertainty within this text? Well, it's aimed at people who either already believe in the magical influence of numbers on their lives or else are contemplating the possibility of such an influence. Either way these people may come from a variety of backgrounds and be living very different lives. Apart from the first sentence of the text, which is general in nature but unlikely to be contested by its readers, the rest has somehow to relate at some point to individual readers. Clearly it can do this only by a lack of definiteness and by merely suggesting the *possibility* of various past events or likely personal reactions. The way in which the text presents these possibilities is largely through the repeated use of the auxiliary verbs *may, can* and *could,* grammatical function words that fundamentally affect the meaning of the text.

COMMENTARY
On Activity 48

You should have found that some modal auxiliaries can express more than one meaning. For instance, 'Xavier and Xanthe can make meringues' could indicate that they have the ability to make them or that they have been given permission to make them; 'Xavier and Xanthe must make meringues' could indicate insistence that they make them, a certainty that they do in fact make them, or an obligation on their part to make them. And so on. You should also have discovered that 'will' can express certainty, intention or insistence in addition to its other common function of indicating future tense. Of course with an isolated sentence it isn't possible to identify one meaning unambiguously. In order to be certain you would in practice need to rely on the context: the surrounding text for instance, or the tone of voice. You can't therefore equate any one auxiliary with just one meaning – this is what makes them so versatile and productive.

Summary

In this chapter you have:

- learned the central importance of the verb in a sentence
- developed an appreciation of the ways in which grammatical choices crucially affect meaning
- found and analysed your own texts for significant verbal patterns.

6 Beyond the Sentence

In this chapter you will:

- discover a grammar for stretches of language larger than the sentence
- distinguish four types of linguistic link used to connect texts
- develop a system for identifying and analysing these links
- apply your grammatical skills to a wide range of texts.

We'll throw the book at you!

Let's first look at a short text that you should certainly feel confident to explore in terms of topics covered in previous chapters. Text 32 (overleaf) is the first page from the *Soldier's Service and Pay Book*, issued to British soldiers during World War II. It served as a record of personal details (such as rank, military training, health and next-of-kin) and also included a form for making a will while on active service.

ACTIVITY 51

1 In pairs or small groups, read Text 32 on the following page and identify all the *grammatical* features that contribute to its high level of formality. (You might, for example, examine the use of the passive voice and modal auxiliaries.)
2 In larger groups, compare your findings and reach agreement. What strikes you as particularly unusual in the wording of this Text?

You should read the commentary on this Activity at the end of the chapter before reading on.

TEXT 32

Army Book 64 (Part I).

Soldier's Service Book.

(Soldier's Pay Book, Army Book 64 (Part II), will be
issued for active service.)

Entries in this book (other than those connected
with the making of a Soldier's Will and insertion of
the names of relatives) are to be made under the
superintendence of an Officer.

Instructions to Soldier.

1. You are held personally responsible for the safe
custody of this book.

2. You will always carry this book on your person.

3. You must produce the book whenever called
upon to do so by a competent military authority, *viz.*,
Officer, Warrant Officer, N.C.O. or Military Policeman.

4. You must not alter or make any entry in this
book (except as regards your next-of-kin on pages 10
and 11 or your Will on pages 15 to 20).

5. Should you lose the book, you will report the
matter to your immediate military superior.

6. On your transfer to the Army Reserve this
book will be handed into your Orderly Room for
transmission, through the O. i|c Records, to place of
rejoining on mobilization.

7. You will be permitted to retain this book after
discharge, but should you lose the book after discharge
it cannot be replaced.

8. If you are discharged from the Army Reserve,
this book will be forwarded to you by the O. i|c
Records.

This page may be photocopied.

Revealing textual patterns

Everything you've so far studied in this book has revolved around the
sentence. This is only to be expected as traditionally grammar has been
concerned almost exclusively with structures no larger than this. For
grammatical purposes the sentence has been the central unit of language.
However, if we never look beyond the sentence level, our understanding of
a text will be rather limited. In order to communicate information or ideas
clearly, writers must surely have some control over how their sentences are
connected to one another in sequence. Now in practice, we haven't
completely ignored this aspect of texts; we've frequently been able to

summarise our findings about individual sentences where we've discovered specific recurring characteristics. Look back for instance to the commentaries to Activity 38 on Text 25 (page 71) and to Activity 46 on Text 29 (page 80). And we've also examined the relationship between Given and New information from one sentence to the next (page 48). But we haven't focused primarily on the links *between* sentences.

If we return to Text 32, now that we've examined it quite closely, we'll find ourselves in a better position to comment on how this text is constructed so that it hangs together as a single piece of writing. We've already remarked on how each sentence is very much self-contained in its repetitive use of words like 'you' and 'book'. But paradoxically this repetition also serves to tie the separate sentences together. It's fairly obvious that in each sentence 'you' and 'your' refer to the same person (the soldier whose book it is), and that 'book' refers to the book in which the text appears. Each of the eight instructions contains at least one mention of both the owner (by the pronoun 'you' or determiner 'your') and the object (by the noun 'book'). These two devices run through the text like two threads, weaving a pattern that is simple, immediately recognisable and strong. The separate sentences are bound together so that 'you' and the 'book' will also be inseparable!

ACTIVITY 52

1 Take a photocopy of Text 32 so that you can use it as a worksheet.
2 On your own, circle or highlight every reference to the book's owner. Now join all these references by drawing a continuous line through the Text.
3 Using a different colour, circle or highlight every mention of the book itself (whether as a noun or by a pronoun), and again draw a line through the Text so that they are all linked.
4 In pairs or as a group, check that you've not omitted any links. You now have a useful visual pattern of the two key interlacing threads in this Text.

Gluing the sentences together

The colligation of grammatical features in Text 32 is predictably regular and not especially sophisticated, but it's certainly adequate for the purpose of conveying meaning to a large group of soldiers from widely differing educational backgrounds. **Cohesion**, which we briefly introduced at the end of Chapter 3 (page 49), is the term used to describe the ways in which language is used to construct an internally unified text and hold it together. You could perhaps picture cohesion as a kind of textual glue. We'd therefore describe Text 32 as being cohesive through its consistent use of the grammatical patterns we've identified.

Here are a couple of further texts for examination. Firstly, Text 33, which is the opening of the section on 'Fainting' from the *Traveller's First Aid Handbook* produced by Reader's Digest.

TEXT 33

Fainting

[1]If the blood supply to the brain is suddenly and temporarily reduced a person may faint. [2]Fainting is usually the result of the victim being in a hot, stuffy atmosphere. [3]But an emotional stimulus, such as an unpleasant sight, a fright or bad news, can also cause fainting. [4]So can a drop in blood sugar due to missed meals or dieting, or standing still for long periods of time. [5]Sometimes there may be a more serious cause, such as illness or injury – in which case a doctor should be consulted.

[6]Someone who is standing still for a long time can reduce the risk of fainting by rocking gently from the heels to the balls of the feet. [7]If someone is about to faint he should sit down. [8]You should loosen tight clothing at the neck and waist and put his head down to his knees.

ACTIVITY 53

1 In small groups, examine the eight sentences in Text 33, which have been numbered for ease of reference. How exactly are these sentences linked to one another? To answer this you will need to adopt a systematic approach:

a Taking each sentence in turn, carefully distinguish the Given information from the New.

b Identify how the Given information is referred to in subsequent sentences.

2 List all the grammatical subjects in the sentences. Discuss to what extent they refer to Given or New information.

3 On your own, rewrite the text so that the grammatical subject of every sentence refers only to Given information, and the remainder of every sentence refers only to New information. In pairs, exchange your versions and discuss them critically.

You should read the commentary on this Activity at the end of the chapter before reading on.

The commentary to Activity 53 may have seemed very detailed in its discussion, but this demonstrates just how *grammatical* choices affect fundamentally the meaning conveyed by language. Though word choice is important, the stylistic fingerprints of a writer become far more apparent from a close examination of the grammatical patterns that are woven through a text. Now on to Text 34, the opening of the chapter on 'Towns' from *Viking Age England* by Julian Richards.

TEXT 34

[1]The Viking Age witnessed an explosion in the development of towns. [2]At the start of the period there may have been less than a dozen places, all trading sites, which we would regard as urban centres. [3]By 1066 there were more than 100 places with some claim to be regarded as towns. [4]Nevertheless, they still contained only a fraction of the population, perhaps some 10 per cent. [5]They included a great diversity of forms, from those that were little more than fortified royal estate centres such as Stafford, to massive cosmopolitan emporia such as York. [6]Nonetheless, most had a Domesday population of more than 1000, with the larger towns such as Lincoln and Norwich having over 5000 townsfolk.

[7]How far was the growth of trading and market sites a result of Viking stimulus, and how far was the development of fortified towns a reaction to the Viking threat? [8]Did the Scandinavian settlers establish any towns of their own? [9]Would towns have developed anyway, if there had been no Scandinavian influence? [10]Was there anything particularly Scandinavian about the character of the towns or their defences? [11]Excavations within many English towns and cities over the last two decades may mean that we are now closer to answering these questions.

ACTIVITY 54

1 On your own, examine the eleven sentences in Text 34, which have again been numbered for ease of reference. List the words or phrases that serve to tie the sentences together into a cohesive whole.

2 If you copy the text, you can use an additional method to reveal the patterns. Circle or highlight these words or phrases and then link them by drawing a continuous line through the Text, in a manner similar to that suggested in Activity 52.

3 In small groups, compare your findings. What types of link does this writer use? Why do you think they are suited to his purpose in writing?

Now read the commentary at the end of the chapter before reading on.

Interlacing links

If you've attempted just one of the last two Activities you'll have begun to appreciate the variety of grammatical patterning possible within a text. You'll also have realised how the comprehensive groundwork on sentence structure that you've covered in earlier chapters is a prerequisite for analysis on this larger scale. You shouldn't lose sight of that valuable early connection we made between texts and textiles (page 6). Grammatical patterning can be woven in as many different ways as there are types of text. However, a text doesn't consist merely of a string of sentences combining to make some sort of 'super-sentence'. On the contrary, it's an integrated unit that reveals its particular meaning through its unique combination of links between sentences. This is why a text is described as a semantic (i.e. concerned with meaning) rather than a grammatical unit, though ironically it is the grammar that contributes significantly towards that meaning.

Unravelling links

A detailed grammatical analysis will uncover types of cohesive device within a text, and will help explain how the text attempts to convey certain meanings and achieve certain objectives. But in order to apply your grammatical knowledge effectively, you must adopt a suitably systematic approach. You can't select just those links that take your personal fancy like a 'pick 'n' mix', or else you may miss some crucial elements within the text. Let's therefore first review the main types of link possible, and then devise a systematic method of application.

There are four main types of cohesive link that can be used to tie sentences together.

1   *Reference*

Reference consists of words and phrases whose meaning can be discovered only by searching elsewhere in the text. In themselves they have very little meaning, but they refer to something else which *does* have identifiable meaning. In the main, reference is represented by pronouns (see page 54), demonstrative determiners (page 55) and occasionally by adverbs relating to place. So for example:

a   Barnaby tossed ten pancakes for Edith. *She* applauded *this* feat and later shared *them* with *him* for supper.
b   Edith sent three sticks of rock to her nice nephew in Knutsford. *These* finally arrived *there* on Saturday.

These straightforward examples also demonstrate another feature of reference, which is that normally it is to something mentioned *previously*. Reference does not usually introduce New information, it repeats Given information. It would certainly be very strange to reverse this pattern, as in

c   Edith sent these to her nice nephew there. Three sticks of rock arrived in Knutsford on Saturday.

Reference back to something previously mentioned is called **anaphoric** reference, and as we've just seen it's the normal pattern in texts. Yet reference *forward*, though unusual, is quite possible:

d   I don't believe *it*! Edith has eaten all the maple syrup pancakes.

Here the meaning of 'it' – the fact that Edith has indeed eaten the pancakes – is revealed only in the second sentence. Such reference forward is called **cataphoric** reference.

2   *Conjunction*

Conjunction (literally a 'joining together') was traditionally a grammatical term for a wide range of linking words, including what we now call coordinators and subordinators (page 56). It's still occasionally used to refer specifically to coordinators, but in the light of more recent advances in analysis it's sensible to avoid confusion by using the term conjunction only for the type of sentence link that we'll now discuss. Whereas 'reference' is largely a matter of simply repeating or re-establishing the specific identity of someone or something under discussion, as in sentences **a** and **b** above, conjunction explains *how* what follows is connected to what precedes. Essentially, conjunction can be subdivided into four main categories. You don't need to worry about their names; it's far more important to appreciate their scope. The four categories, with examples, are:

■ **Additive**: links that add similar or non-contradictory information

(e.g. *and, and also, in addition, furthermore, besides, in other words, nor, likewise*)

- **Adversative**: links that supply contrasting or unexpected information
  (e.g. *but, yet, however, nevertheless, although, unless, until, on the other hand, despite this, on the contrary*)

- **Temporal**: links that express a relation of time
  (e.g. *then, previously, subsequently, next, after, meanwhile, firstly, secondly, finally, at the same time, at last*)

- **Causal**: links that express reason, purpose or result
  (e.g. *so, consequently, because, as a result, therefore, in the circumstances, then, on account of*).

And here's a short example of these various conjunctive links in practice:

e   Edith had loved maple syrup pancakes for breakfast. *And indeed* she had *also* loved them for lunch and tea. *However*, she no longer relishes them very much at any meal. *Previously* she had indulged herself all day long. *As a result* she had been as sick as a dog.

If we examine the examples under each of the four subdivisions above, we can see something of the range of conjunctive links possible. Two important points to note are:

- conjunction can be represented by one word or a group of words
- conjunction cannot be equated with a particular class of word.

You can see just from the small selection listed above that conjunction can include all three types of connective (page 56) as well as prepositional phrases (page 57). Here are just a few examples:

Coordinators: *and, nor, but, yet.*

Subordinators: *although, unless, until, after, because.*

Conjuncts: *however, subsequently, meanwhile, consequently.*

Prepositional phrases: *in other words, on the contrary, at the same time.*

What's important yet again is not the class of word but the *function* of the word or group of words in context.

3   *Ellipsis*

Ellipsis is an extremely common yet very much overlooked feature of language, particularly in speech. In fact we've already had cause to examine it a number of times already (pages 9 and 21). Technically, ellipsis is the omission of a word or words without any consequent loss of meaning. You might think it strange that the absence of something could have a positive and cohesive effect on a text, but this initial and quite natural reaction underlines just how much we underestimate the part we play as readers or listeners. More often than not, something isn't said or stated because it simply isn't necessary; it's understood by the reader or listener from the context. So for instance:

f   Rosamund couldn't decide which bonnet to buy. Eventually she chose the prettiest.

g   Sigismund was laughing. Rosamund wasn't.

h   Sigismund declared to Rosamund that he loved the bonnet. In reality, of course, he didn't.

These three examples demonstrate different levels of ellipsis. Example **f** omits the noun 'bonnet' (the implied object) from the second sentence; **g** omits a second mention of the main verb 'laughing', relying solely on the auxiliary verb and attached negative for the implied meaning; and **h** omits the main verb 'loved' and noun phrase 'the bonnet', again indicating the complete meaning by the combined auxiliary and negative 'didn't'. Try writing out these examples without any ellipsis and notice how awkward and stilted they become.

Grammatical structures from the single word to more complex units can therefore be omitted, yet be clearly implied by the preceding text. We reconstruct the missing grammatical elements from our understanding of earlier sentences. In fact it's actually unusual to continually mention everything in an explicit fashion, as you can see from two earlier texts which do just that: Texts 16 and 32. These texts were deliberately written in an extremely explicit manner so that their intended readers could be left in no possible doubt about their meaning. But in most cases a writer or speaker can rely to a greater extent on the reader or listener to 'fill in the gaps'. This, of course, is an essential part of the whole interactive or two-way process in communicating through language.

4   *Lexical cohesion*

As the name implies, this type of link is more to do with vocabulary (lexis) than with grammar, though this is arguably more a matter of degree rather than of absolute distinction. However, regardless of how far it may be lexical or grammatical, we need to examine it in order to complete our survey of the main cohesive devices. **Lexical cohesion** is concerned with content words (nouns, verbs, adjectives and adverbs), not function words. It's about the lexical choices that writers and speakers make to tie their separate sentences and utterances together. Lexical cohesion can be subdivided into two types.

Firstly, **reiteration**: the repetition of meaning by various related content words. This can be achieved in a number of ways. An example will help make this clear:

i   [1]The *boy* sat down at the table. [2]Slowly the *boy* poured the thick maple syrup over the pancakes. [3]The *lad* was obviously intending to relish this meal. [4]Being a greedy *child*, he had an appetite far larger than he could comfortably satisfy. [5]He was a *glutton*.

In each sentence the same person is mentioned but in diverse ways. Sentence 2 displays the simplest and most obvious way by merely repeating the same word; sentence 3 uses a **synonym** (a word with the same or a similar meaning); sentence 4 uses a more general but clearly related word; and sentence 5 uses another general but this time unrelated word. The crucial difference between sentences 4 and 5 is that whereas a boy or lad is also a child, he is a glutton only in this particular context. Example **i** therefore shows something of the variation possible with nouns, but such variation can apply equally to the three other classes of content word.

Secondly, **collocation**: the tendency of words and phrases to occur together. We've already come across this important linguistic feature in Chapter 3 (page 40), where we introduced the corresponding grammatical concept of colligation. Text 9 (page 20) provides a straightforward example. Reading a text entitled 'The weather today', we can feel confident in predicting that this topic will be maintained through the regular recurrence of words and phrases relating to the weather and to specific geographical areas. In other words, we expect to meet with a selection from the total set of possible words relating to these aspects of the environment. And so we do. In the first few lines we come across 'cloudy', 'fair', 'rain', 'sunny spells' and 'wind', as well as 'north of Scotland', 'western coastal areas', 'Central Highlands' and 'Argyll'. Obviously the words and phrases in both sets are not in any way synonyms; they refer to very different though ultimately related things. They are therefore examples of collocation, not reiteration.

Electrifying links

The links that a writer chooses will not only reflect the type of text but also represent an integral part of its meaning. It's therefore essential that you identify them in a systematic and comprehensive manner rather than by a subjective 'hit and miss' approach. Only by a careful and methodical examination can you successfully discover the particular stylistic fingerprints of a writer. Here then is a system for locating and identifying the chain of links within a text. Let's first choose a text, in this case the opening two paragraphs from an introductory non-specialist article on the nineteenth-century scientist Michael Faraday, published in the 1990s.

TEXT 35

[1]It is almost impossible, now, for us to imagine a world without electricity. [2]We almost take it for granted that lighting, communications, transport, cooking and entertainment will all be available at the flick of a switch, and we only realise how much we depend upon electricity on those rare occasions when the power fails and all the services of a town come to a halt.

[3]At the beginning of the last century electricity could only be produced from primitive batteries. [4]It was still a laboratory curiosity, until Faraday made the first dynamo, transformer and electric motor. [5]His discoveries were not applied practically until some years after his death, but his work had pointed the way forward to the large-scale generation of electric power, and all that was later to come from this. [6]In a very real sense Michael Faraday helped to make the world as we know it today. [7]This is his most obvious achievement, but he made very

important contributions to many other areas of physics and chemistry and his lesser achievements tend to be overshadowed: for example, he was the first person to liquefy chlorine and to make a detailed investigation of several chemicals, such as benzene. [8]His stature, as one of the world's greatest scientists, and perhaps the greatest scientific educator of the nineteenth century, is all the more remarkable if we consider his origins.

This introduction consists of eight sentences. We need to map the various links under the following headings:

Sentence Number	Linguistic Item	Related Item	Sentence Number	Type

This is how you use the table. Beginning with sentence 2, the number of which you place in the first column, you search for any word or phrase that links in some way to sentence 1. All words and phrases are together labelled as 'linguistic items', in other words items or components of language. Those you find in sentence 2 are placed in the second column; the connected items that you identify in sentence 1 you place in the third column. In the fourth column you place the number of the sentence in which you found the related items. Finally, in the fifth column, you identify the type of link for each separate item (i.e. reference, conjunction, ellipsis, or lexical cohesion). You then move on to sentence 3 and repeat the procedure.

Let's see how it works in practice. Under the last column, the various types have been abbreviated: Reference to Ref, Conjunction to Con; Lexical cohesion to LC.

Sentence Number	Linguistic Item	Related Item	Sentence Number	Type
2	We ($\times$ 3)	us	1	Ref
2	lighting	electricity	1	LC
2	communications	electricity	1	LC
2	transport	electricity	1	LC
2	cooking	electricity	1	LC
2	entertainment	electricity	1	LC
2	flick of a switch	electricity	1	LC
2	electricity	electricity	1	LC
2	power	electricity	1	LC
3	At the beginning of the last century	now	1	Con
3	electricity	electricity	2	LC
3	batteries	electricity	2	LC
4	It	electricity	3	Ref

Continued

Sentence Number	Linguistic Item	Related Item	Sentence Number	Type
4	dynamo	electricity	3	LC
4	transformer	electricity	3	LC
4	electric motor	electricity	3	LC
5	His (× 2)	Faraday	4	Ref
5	discoveries	dynamo, transformer and electric motor	4	LC
5	work	(ditto)	4	LC
5	electric power	(ditto)	4	LC
5	later	At the beginning of the last century	3	Con

Although we've examined only five sentences, the number of links may well have surprised you. But first let's note some important general points that apply to all texts:

- Cohesion assumes that texts move regularly from Given information to New; consequently, to uncover the links, you always work *back* to previous sentences. You therefore start with the *second* sentence.
- Sentences usually contain a number of cohesive links. As a rule, the higher the number, the more easily understandable is the text.
- Although in the first instance you are looking to connect a sentence to the immediately previous one, links are not always so consistently consecutive. Some sentences may not contain any link with the immediately previous one, in which case you'll need to continue working back through earlier sentences. You'll find that several sentences will contain links only with some of these earlier ones. Some sentences, of course, will contain a mixture of links with both the immediately previous sentence and the more remote ones.
- Once you've made a link with an earlier link, it's unnecessary to go back further. For example, in Text 35 the word 'electricity' is one link between sentences 3 and 2. You don't need to list the link for the same word between sentences 3 and 1, because you've already recorded the word as a link between sentences 2 and 1. You've therefore established a connecting chain of links that reveals part of the text's patterning.
- As far as possible you should record *every* link you can detect, otherwise you won't be able to see the complete pattern. So again in Text 35, all three occurrences of 'we' in sentence 2 are listed.

Weighing up the chain

The exercise of tabulating the cohesive links within a text is potentially a very useful piece of evidence for understanding and assessing a text. However, you shouldn't see such an analysis in itself as in any sense an interpretation of the text. In other words, it isn't an interpretation of what the text means but it can provide an explanation of how and why it means what it does. It's *one* way of raising to a conscious level our intuitions about how a text works.

If we now examine our tabulation of the first five sentences from Text 35, we can already make some useful observations even though the exercise is incomplete. For instance:

- Lexical cohesion is by far the most prominent type of link, occurring several times in each sentence. The topic in this section of the text is unmistakably electricity itself rather than the man Faraday. A more detailed examination would reveal that collocation is the more frequent form of lexical cohesion.
- Of the other types of link, reference occurs occasionally, while the two examples of conjunction serve to make links between sentences that aren't consecutive. Ellipsis plays no role at this stage.

We can see how this type of text relies upon such links. The opening paragraphs set the scene by establishing the topic and demonstrating its wide-ranging importance and application through the use of lexical cohesion, especially collocation. The topic is reinforced by the frequency of such links. The writer needs to make the nature and scope of his article clear; in addition, he doesn't assume that his audience has any appreciable amount of shared knowledge about the early history of electricity. Therefore he doesn't use ellipsis. On the other hand, he does initially use the first person plural ('us' and 'we') as a means of creating a relationship between the reader and himself, and by extension between the reader and the world of electricity. You should now feel confident not only to complete the last three sentences of Text 35, but also to tackle any other text you may encounter.

ACTIVITY 55

1 Either on your own or in pairs, complete the analysis of sentences 6–8 of Text 35.
2 In larger groups, compare your tables and agree your analysis. How do the links you have found affect the observations made earlier about the first five sentences? How would you now characterise the topic of the Text?

ACTIVITY 56

1 On your own, write four consecutive sentences that contain *no* cohesive links between them.
2 Next in pairs, exchange your four sentences and examine each other's. Can you detect any links? If not, do you think the four sentences constitute a text?
3 As a class, discuss your findings. How do you recognise a text as a text?

An alternative discovery method

The next text is constructed in a slightly different manner. It's a section from Jostein Gaarder's introduction to philosophy, *Sophie's World*, a book that popularises the subject for the general reader. In the following extract the author is discussing the method of inquiry employed by the Greek philosopher Socrates.

TEXT 36

[1]The essential nature of Socrates' art lay in the fact that he did not appear to want to instruct people. [2]On the contrary he gave the impression of one desiring to learn from those he spoke with. So instead of lecturing like a traditional schoolmaster, he *discussed*.

[3]Obviously he would not have become a famous philosopher had he confined himself purely to listening to others. [4]Nor would he have been sentenced to death. [5]But he just asked questions, especially to begin a conversation, as if he knew nothing. [6]In the course of the discussion he would generally get his opponents to recognize the weakness of their arguments, and, forced into a corner, they would finally be obliged to realize what was right and what was wrong.

[7]Socrates, whose mother was a midwife, used to say that his art was like the art of the midwife. [8]She does not herself give birth to the child, but she is there to help during its delivery. [9]Similarly, Socrates saw his task as helping people to 'give birth' to the correct insight, since real understanding must come from within. [10]It cannot be imparted by someone else. [11]And only the understanding that comes from within can lead to true insight.

[12]Let me put it more precisely: The ability to give birth is a natural characteristic. [13]In the same way, everybody can grasp philosophical truths if they just use their innate reason. [14]Using your innate reason means reaching down inside yourself and using what is there.

[15]By playing ignorant, Socrates forced the people he met to use their common sense. [16]Socrates could feign ignorance – or pretend to be dumber than he was. [17]We call this Socratic irony.

ACTIVITY 57

1 On your own, using a table like the one suggested on page 98, analyse the links between the sentences in Text 36.

2 In what ways are the links different from those in Text 35? Why has the writer chosen these links for the Text?

Now that you've examined a few texts in considerable detail, you can appreciate how the types of link actually convey much of the meaning in a text. Any text will display types of link in a particular combination. The particular aspects to consider in each case are:

■ The frequency of each type of link. A basic distinction between reference, conjunction, ellipsis and lexical cohesion is a good starting point, but often it's also insightful to discriminate further (e.g. between kinds of conjunction or between reiteration and collocation).

■ The proportion of the types relative to one another. Is there, for instance, a predominance of one type, or even a complete absence?

■ The density of the links. How often does a type of link occur between any two sentences? Is there a concentration of links in any part of the text?

In this way you will be identifying some of the colligational stylistic fingerprints of a text. In other words, you will uncover how *meaning is structured*.

ACTIVITY 58

1 On your own, find a type of text that you commonly read or are familiar with. Examples might include adverts, music reviews, feature articles from magazines or newspapers, and recipes. Analyse a representative sample – say a dozen sentences – using the tabular layout.
2 Next calculate in turn the frequency, relative proportions and density of the links you've uncovered. How do these aspects contribute to the meaning of the text? To what extent are they a necessary characteristic of the type of text you've chosen?
3 Bring your text to class and present your findings, either to a group or to the whole class.

ACTIVITY 59

1 On your own, perhaps as a development of the previous Activity, you could undertake a longer-term investigative project. For instance, choose two or three texts from the same genre (e.g. holiday brochures, agony aunt letters, or adverts) sharing the same topic but aimed at different target audiences.
2 Analyse representative extracts from each and compare your findings. Write a suitable report or essay in which you present, discuss and interpret the results.
3 Alternatively, see if you can find some old school exercise books from two or more years ago. Choose a passage that's similar to something that you've written recently, and analyse both for the types of link you've used. What types predominate in each? To what extent has your writing style changed?

Journalistic time warps

In Chapter 4 (page 62) we examined a piece of typical tabloid journalism for some specific grammatical features. News reporting often displays a number of unusual linguistic features, many of them grammatical. The following Text is the first section of a report from the Daily Mail of 27 December 2000 about a violent incident in the USA. All but one of the paragraphs consist of a single sentence.

TEXT 37

Terror at Internet firm as worker shoots seven

From **Annette Witheridge** in New York

A DISGRUNTLED employee calmly got up from his desk at an Internet company and shot dead seven of his colleagues yesterday.

Staff believed he feared he was about to lose his job in a wave of redundancies caused by the collapse of the Internet boom.

Michael McDermott, 42, armed with a Kalashnikov AK 37, a semi automatic and a shotgun, methodically picked off his victims in the open plan office in Massachusetts an hour after starting work as normal.

Police later overpowered him as he sat with his weapons in the lobby of the firm, Edgewater Technology at Wakefield, near Boston.

Colleagues said the company was planning to make 25 people redundant in the New Year and McDermott, who started work there only ten months ago, was afraid he would be one of the first to go.

Between 30 and 40 staff were believed to be inside the building, a converted mill, when McDermott got up from his desk and launched the murderous attack.

As they cowered in corners and dived under desks many managed to call police from mobile phones.

Some were ushered out of a back door and into a nearby church for safety. Several were treated for shock and counsellors were on hand to help workers come to terms with what had happened.

SWAT teams were on hand but officers – who were last night still searching the building for clues – called them off once it became clear there was only one gunman.

District Attorney John McAvoy refused to reveal details of the victims until relatives had been notified.

ACTIVITY 60

1 On your own, list the cohesive links between the sentences, using the tabular method described on page 98.

2 What is the predominant type of link and why?

3 Next examine the use of temporal conjunction (i.e. the relation to time – see page 95) throughout the text. What does this reveal about the narrative structure of the report, in other words the order in which the sequence of events is reported?

4 In class, compare your findings and discuss possible reasons for the discoveries you've made about the ordering of events in a news story.

5 On your own, as an investigative project, find news reports of the same story in two or three different newspapers on the same day, and examine the temporal conjunctive links. To what extent are the patterns similar or dissimilar?

Another electrifying experience!

And finally one more text for analysis. This is the opening of the semi-autobiographical novel *The Bell Jar* by the American writer Sylvia Plath.

TEXT 38

[1]It was a queer, sultry summer, the summer they electrocuted the Rosenburgs, and I didn't know what I was doing in New York. [2]I'm stupid about executions. [3]The idea of being electrocuted makes me sick, and that's all there was to read about in the papers – goggle-eyed headlines staring up at me on every street corner and at the fusty, peanut-smelling mouth of every subway. [4]It had nothing to do with me, but I couldn't help wondering what it would be like, being burned alive all along your nerves.

[5]I thought it must be the worst thing in the world.

[6]New York was bad enough. [7]By nine in the morning the fake, country-wet freshness that somehow seeped in overnight evaporated like the tail end of a sweet dream. [8]Mirage-grey at the bottom of their granite canyons, the hot streets wavered in the sun, the car tops sizzled and glittered, and the dry, cindery dust blew into my eyes and down my throat.

[9]I kept hearing about the Rosenburgs over the radio and at the office till I couldn't get them out of my mind. [10]It was like the first time I saw a cadaver. [11]For weeks afterwards, the cadaver's head – or what there was left of it – floated up behind my eggs and bacon at breakfast and behind the face of Buddy Willard, who was responsible for my seeing it in the first place, and pretty soon I felt as though I were carrying that cadaver's head around with me on a string, like some black, noseless balloon stinking of vinegar.

[12]I knew something was wrong with me that summer, because all I could think about was the Rosenburgs and how stupid I'd been to buy all those uncomfortable, expensive clothes, hanging limp as fish in my closet, and how all the little successes I'd totted up so happily at college fizzled to nothing outside the slick marble and plate-glass fronts along Madison Avenue.

ACTIVITY 61

1 Either on your own or in pairs, analyse the links in Text 38 by using the tabular method described on page 98. Then calculate the frequency, relative proportions and density of the links.

2 In groups or as a class, compare your findings. What do they tell you about the meaning of the text?

3 If you now re-examine the text, you'll probably find that there remain some portions for which no obvious links exist. Do you think any of these unconnected portions might be significant in any way? Discuss why you haven't found any clear links relating them to the rest of the text.

When you have completed this Activity, read the very detailed commentary at the end of the chapter.

COMMENTARY
On Activity 51

Some of the grammatical features that you should have noted as contributing to the text's formality are:

■ The use of the passive voice in the introductory paragraph ('are to be made') and in instruction numbers 1 ('are held'), 3 ('called upon'), 6 ('will be handed'), 7 ('will be permitted' and 'cannot be replaced') and 8 ('are discharged' and 'will be forwarded').

■ The deliberate choice of modal auxiliaries to convey insistence and obligation ('will' in instruction numbers 2 and 5; 'must' in numbers 3 and 4). Note also that 'will' in instruction numbers 7 and 8 combines the expression of future tense with the modality of certainty.

- The first subject of each instruction, apart from number 6, is 'You', which occurs as either the first or second word. (The second word of instruction 6 is the related determiner 'your'.)
- Every sentence is self-contained in that each refers explicitly to 'this book' or 'the book'; no sentence relies on the mention of the book in earlier sentences by simply using the pronoun 'it'.

This particular pattern of grammatical features, this colligation, conveys a strong sense of formality, reinforced by the choice of a polysyllabic and Latinate vocabulary (e.g. 'superintendence', 'transmission', 'mobilization') as well as impersonal and legalistic phrasing (e.g. 'safe custody', 'on your person'). In this context the use of the second person pronoun 'you' may be personal but it isn't very friendly. And though all sentences are declaratives, their combined force is of commands rather than mere statements, resulting from the modal auxiliaries employed and the similarity in structure that several instructions display (e.g. in the repetitive first subject 'You'). The soldier concerned will certainly interpret the heading 'Instructions' as also meaning 'Commands'!

Overall, one of the most unusual features is contained in the last bullet point above: the repetitive reference to 'book' by the same word rather than pronominally (i.e. by using a pronoun). This repetition, especially when accompanied by the demonstrative determiner 'this' (see page 55), serves to indicate that the book is the key topic of the text, even though in most cases it isn't the grammatical subject of a clause. There are a number of terms to describe this emphasis. We can speak generally of **foregrounding**: any use of language that is in some way unusual in context so as to attract attention. This very useful word is borrowed from painting, where things in the foreground of a picture are more prominent than those in the background. (The cleft sentence construction that we examined on page 84 is an example of grammatical foregrounding.) However, in this particular case, the same feature is consistently foregrounded a number of times. The cumulative effect is to assert the 'book' as the **topic** or theme of the text, and so we can speak here of its **topicalisation** (or **thematisation**). We've seen earlier (page 18) that although the topic of a sentence is by no means always the same thing as the subject, it very often is. Sentences tend to start from the Given (i.e. information already provided to or known by the reader or speaker) and move to the New. Grammatical subjects also tend to appear at the beginning of sentences and represent the Given. But this common pattern can be altered for any number of reasons, and in this case the writer of Text 32 has chosen to foreground and topicalise the 'book', while at the same time making clear that obligations fall upon the grammatical subject 'you'.

Text 33 is first repeated here with the Given information emboldened.

Fainting

¹If the blood supply to the brain is suddenly and temporarily reduced **a person may faint**. ²**Fainting** is usually the result of **the victim** being in a hot, stuffy atmosphere. ³But an emotional stimulus, such as an unpleasant sight, a fright or bad news, **can also cause fainting**. ⁴**So can** a drop in blood sugar due to missed meals or dieting, or standing still for long periods of time. ⁵**Sometimes there may be a** more serious **cause**, such as illness or injury – in which case a doctor should be consulted.

⁶**Someone who is standing still for a long time** can reduce the risk of fainting by rocking gently from the heels to the balls of the feet. ⁷If **someone is about to faint** he should sit down. ⁸You should loosen tight clothing at the neck and waist and put **his head** down to his knees.

You should be able to trace the emboldened Given information to an earlier mention within the text. So in

Sentence 1:   **a person may faint** merely expands the section heading **Fainting**

Sentence 2:   both **Fainting** and **the victim** effectively repeat **a person may faint**

Sentence 3:   **can also cause fainting** refers again to **Fainting** as well as to the particular cause (by the word **also**) described in sentence 2

Sentence 4:   **So can** is an alternative way of expressing **can also cause fainting**

Sentence 5:   **Sometimes there may be a [...] cause** is a general phrase that alludes to the various causes mentioned in earlier sentences

Sentence 6:   **Someone who is standing still for a long time** echoes the phrase 'standing still for long periods of time' in sentence 4, and also relates to **a person** and **the victim** earlier

Sentence 7:   **If someone is about to faint** repeats **Someone** and relates to the general theme in the Text of the causes of fainting

Sentence 8:   **his head** refers to **someone**.

This exercise allows us to see how New information is integrated with Given to create a pattern within the Text. In addition, it reveals some of the links between the sentences, but only *some*. The obvious ones are in the repetition of nouns or verbs, or short phrases containing them. There's also occasional variation in the noun chosen, e.g. **person** and **victim**, while subsequent mention is by the pronoun **Someone**.

But apart from this reliance on repeated Given information, the writer also uses other devices to make the text cohesive, for example:

■ the connective 'But' (specifically a coordinator – see page 56) is used at the beginning of sentence 3
■ the connective 'So' is used at the beginning of sentence 4 to mean 'in additon'; the following 'can' implies 'also cause fainting' in the previous sentence

- though 'Sometimes' at the beginning of sentence 5 is an adverb, it functions here as a link between two ideas: the previously established fact that various causes of fainting exist and the further fact that there can be 'more serious' causes.

The important thing is to recognise the ways in which the writer links the sentences together. As long as you're able to identify the words or phrases that serve as these links, don't worry too much if you can't always be sure of the class of word involved. It's more important to recognise the function of a particular word or phrase than to agonise over its form.

The grammatical subjects of the sentences follow; those that refer to Given information are emboldened. You should, of course, have remembered that a sentence can have more than one subject! (see page 28).

Sentence	Subject(s)
1	the blood supply to the brain; **a person**
2	**Fainting**; **the victim**
3	an emotional stimulus
4	a drop in blood sugar due to missed meals or dieting; standing still for long periods of time
5	**there** (see p 42); a doctor
6	**Someone**
7	**someone**; he
8	You

The topic maintained within the text is clearly first the causes of fainting and then its cures, but the above table reveals that the sentences are varied stylistically so that the subject sometimes reinforces Given information and sometimes introduces New information. What's more, although we expect a typical sentence to move from Given to New, we can see that this pattern is here occasionally reversed. The first sentence delays the repetition of information given in the section heading by attracting the reader's attention to some relevant detail; yet the emphasis is placed squarely on the Given by using an opening dependent clause that leads into the main clause 'a person may faint'. You should also notice how sentence 4 reverses the normal SV sequence by placing two quite complicated noun phrases after the verb 'can'. And the last sentence is the first to mention 'You', a neat way to relate everything in the text to the first-aid action that the reader should take. The text achieves its cohesion from a variety of repetitive devices, deliberately chosen to ensure that the reader will understand and be left in no doubt about what action to take in an emergency. If you attempted to rewrite the text as indicated at the end of the Activity, you should have found your version to be rather tedious and awkward in its predictable repetitive structure.

The sentence links you should have identified within the first paragraph are:

Sentence	Link
1	towns
2	At the start of the period
3	By 1066
4	Nevertheless, they
5	They
6	Nonetheless, most

Some simple yet varied devices connect the sentences in the first paragraph of this text. Sentences 2 and 3 begin with adverbials (see page 23) that refer to 'The Viking Age', the subject of the first sentence. This sentence in turn is linked to the chapter title by the word 'towns'. Sentences 4 to 6 use pronouns ('they', 'They' and 'most') to refer to 'places' in sentence 3, but in addition there are two rather different links in sentences 4 and 6. Whereas the adverbials and the pronouns refer to a specific part of an earlier sentence, 'Nevertheless' and 'Nonetheless' each refers to the *total* meaning of the sentence that precedes it, and in addition indicates that a contrast of some kind is about to be presented. This type of connective, the conjunct (page 56), is very useful for linking stretches of prose that develop ideas or present arguments.

The second paragraph is markedly different in its method of linking. At a lexical level each of the five sentences includes the word 'towns' (not always as subject) in order to maintain the general topic. But what adds to the cohesive nature of the sentences is the choice of four interrogatives followed by a final declarative that includes the phrase 'answering these questions'. Taken together, these two types of cohesion clarify the meaning of these introductory paragraphs for the reader. The first outlines some contrasting facts about the topic of towns during the Viking Age; the second poses a number of relevant and related questions, concluding with an indication that the reader will find some answers in the rest of the chapter.

Firstly, let's examine a table of the cohesive links that exist between the twelve sentences in Text 38.

Sentence No.	Linguistic Item	Related Item	Sentence No.	Type
2	I	I (× 2)	1	Ref
2	stupid	didn't know what I was doing	1	LC
2	executions	electrocuted the Rosenburgs	1	LC
3	being electrocuted	executions	2	LC
3	me (× 2)	I	2	Ref
3	goggle-eyed	stupid	2	LC
3	every street corner	New York	1	LC
3	every subway	New York	1	LC
4	It	headlines	3	Ref
4	me	me	3	Ref
4	I	me	3	Ref
4	wondering	idea	3	LC
4	being burned alive	being electrocuted	3	LC
5	I	I	4	Ref
		me	4	Ref
5	thought	wondering	4	LC
5	it	it	4	Ref
		being burned alive	4	Ref
6	New York	every street corner	3	LC
		every subway	4	LC
6	bad enough	worst thing	5	LC
8	Mirage	fake	7	LC
		dream	7	LC
8	hot	sultry	1	LC
		burned	4	LC
8	streets	New York	6	LC
8	sun	summer (× 2)	1	LC
8	car tops	street	3	LC
8	sizzled	burned	4	LC
8	dry	evaporated	6	LC

Sentence No.	Linguistic Item	Related Item	Sentence No.	Type
8	cindery	burned	4	LC
8	my (× 2)	I	5	Ref
9	I (× 2)	my (× 2)	8	Ref
9	the Rosenburgs	the Rosenburgs	1	LC
9	them	the Rosenburgs	1	Ref
9	my	my	8	Ref
9	mind	thought	5	LC
10	It	couldn't get them out of my mind	9	Ref
10	I	I (× 2)	9	Ref
10	cadaver	the Rosenburgs	9	LC
11	For weeks afterwards	the first time	10	Con
11	the cadaver's head	cadaver	10	LC
11	what there was left	cadaver	10	LC
11	it	cadaver	10	Ref
11	in the first place	the first time	10	Con
11	I (× 2)	I	10	Ref
11	that	cadaver	10	Ref
11	cadaver's head	cadaver	10	LC
11	me	I	10	Ref
11	black	cindery	8	LC
11	noseless	cadaver	9	LC
11	stinking	sick	3	LC
		fusty	3	LC
12	I (× 4)	I	11	Ref
12	wrong	queer	1	LC
12	that	summer	1	Ref
12	summer	summer	1	LC
		summer they electrocuted the Rosenburgs	1	LC
12	me	I	11	Ref
12	think about	mind	9	LC
12	the Rosenburgs	the Rosenburgs	9	LC
12	stupid	stupid	2	LC

Sentence No.	Linguistic Item	Related Item	Sentence No.	Type
12	my	I	11	Ref
12	fizzled	sizzled	8	LC
12	marble	granite	8	LC
12	plate-glass fronts	streets	8	LC
12	nothing	nothing	4	LC
12	Madison Avenue	streets	8	LC

Of course it may be that you were able to discover one or two further links, but the above table is fairly comprehensive! On the other hand, don't worry if you missed some. If you were able to identify seventy per cent or so, then you've probably been able to uncover some interesting facts about the text. Here are just a few initial observations:

■ Lexical cohesion comprises the main link (44 items = 56%). A more detailed analysis would reveal that reiteration and collocation are about evenly split.
■ Reference is the other common cohesive link (32 items = 41%). Of these, three-quarters refer to the first person narrator.
■ Conjunction occurs only twice; ellipsis isn't evident, though you could argue that the opening five words of sentence 7 are elliptical by implying 'in New York'.
■ The length of a sentence is no guide to the number of links it contains. At four words, sentence 2 contains four links; at twenty-three words, sentence 7 contains no anaphoric links and is not strongly connected to subsequent sentences.

But how are these observations relevant to the text? How do we interpret them? And how do they contribute to the text's meaning? Well, the predominance of the first-person reference suggests that the narrator's point of view is of primary importance. What's significant here is the density of personal reference in such a short stretch of text, not merely the fact that the first person pronoun occurs. There is relatively little use of reference otherwise, indicating that it's more important to identify things by explicit and descriptive naming. Hence the wealth of lexical cohesion. If in turn we examine these links, we notice a number of patterns emerging. The collocation of 'idea', 'wondering', 'thought', 'mind' and 'think about' is clearly connected to the continual personal reference, and together they suggest the narrator's almost obsessional preoccupation. But one of the most interesting aspects is the way in which burning and heat recur, being connected regularly to both the execution of the Rosenburgs and the New York weather. During the course of the twelve sentences these two images become increasingly interwoven.

The almost complete absence of conjunction means that the reader has often to work out possible connections. Many of the sentences are more concerned with descriptions of events than establishing reasons or causes, though *within* a particular sentence a reason is sometimes provided (e.g.

sentence 12). You could also argue that the lack of ellipsis reflects the narrator's need to clarify everything explicitly. Taken as a whole, the particular mix of cohesive devices suggests a narrator who is introspective, very much concerned with her state of mind, and rather confused. It should come as no surprise to learn that later in the novel the narrator suffers a nervous breakdown.

But establishing the cohesive links between sentences doesn't reveal everything about a text – and isn't intended to. It's just *one* approach out of many, and so needs to be complemented by others for a fuller understanding. This becomes all the clearer when we examine the portions of Text 38 that haven't been linked. Some of these are easily explained, as for example the mention in sentence 11 of 'Buddy Willard', a character who is developed later in the novel. On the other hand, phrases such as 'like the tail end of a sweet [dream]', 'like some [black, noseless] balloon', and 'hanging limp as fish' are either incompletely connected or not at all. We can see why. Being similes they act to compare things that are normally dissimilar or *unconnected*. And this observation brings us back to where we began in this book: with the sentence.

An examination of the structure of each sentence could prove equally enlightening. To take just one example, the very first sentence displays some features that are sufficiently unusual as to be examples of foregrounding (page 105). The clause 'the summer they electrocuted the Rosenburgs' is in apposition to the complement 'a queer, sultry summer', but is foregrounded by its repetition of 'summer', so accentuating this word. In addition, the last two clauses 'I didn't know what I was doing in New York' are connected to the earlier part of the sentence by the coordinator 'and', as if they have roughly the same significance. Yet their content is markedly different and quite unexpected. This is caused partly by the abrupt change of subject to 'I', when it had seemed as if the topic of the sentence, and possibly of the immediately following text also, might well be the 'summer'. In fact, removing those last two clauses alters completely the emphasis in the first paragraph. The topic then becomes the execution of the Rosenburgs rather than the narrator's state of mind.

Clearly it's just as important to look *within* sentences as *between* them. Then we may find an interplay of structures that will reveal quite intricate patterns of meaning, not just a tangle of words. Grammatical knowledge is one of the most powerful keys for unlocking the evidence in texts for the intuitions we sense but often cannot pin down. Grammatical knowledge explains what's going on in a text. You shouldn't worry if you haven't found everything that's discussed in these commentaries; most have been deliberately detailed in order to indicate the potential power of grammar. If you have the basic foundation outlined earlier in this book, you can advance as far as you wish.

Summary

In this chapter you have:

- acquired a system for the analysis of links between sentences
- applied your analytical skills to uncover how meaning is organised in texts
- found and investigated your own texts to develop your understanding.

Appendix: The Textual Kaleidoscope

This appendix provides some further texts for exploration at different levels. No specific Activities are suggested, although there are some suggestions for general approaches. Naturally, all texts here are appropriate for examination of the cohesive devices discussed in Chapter 6.

Text 39 is the opening of *Cages*, a short story by the East African writer Abdulrazak Gurnah. It's suitable for examination at quite an early stage, either while working through Chapter 2 on the subject and the finite verb, or Chapter 3 on kinds of sentence.

TEXT 39

[1]There were times when it felt to Hamid as if he had been in the shop always, and that his life would end there. [2]He no longer felt discomfort, nor did he hear the secret mutterings at the dead hours of night which had once emptied his heart in dread. [3]He knew now that they came from the seasonal swamp which divided the city from the townships, and which teemed with life. [4]The shop was in a good position, at a major crossroads from the city's suburbs. [5]He opened it at first light when the earliest workers were shuffling by, and did not shut it again until all but the last stragglers had trailed home. [6]He liked to say that at his station he saw all of life pass him by. [7]At peak hours he would be on his feet all the time, talking and bantering with the customers, courting them and taking pleasure in the skill with which he handled himself and his merchandise. [8]Later he would sink exhausted on the boxed seat which served as his till.

[9]The girl appeared at the shop late one evening, just as he was thinking it was time to close. [10]He had caught himself nodding twice, a dangerous trick in such desperate times. [11]The second time he had woken up with a start, thinking a large hand was clutching his throat and lifting him off the ground. [12]She was standing in front of him, waiting with a look of disgust in her face.

Text 40 is an extract from Margaret Atwood's historical novel *Alias Grace*, which tells the story of the notorious nineteenth century murderess Grace Marks. This extract begins soon after she has been looking at a scrapbook of famous crimes, kept by the wife of the Penitentiary Governor in charge of her prison. As a first person narrative it can usefully be compared with Texts 4 and 5 in Chapter 1, though more of its particular patterns will only be appreciated after the first three chapters have been completed.

TEXT 40

[1]I'm not looking at the scrapbook now, because they may come in at any moment. [2]I sit with my rough hands folded, eyes down, staring at the flowers in the Turkey carpet. [3]Or they are supposed to be flowers. [4]They have petals the shape of the diamonds on a playing card; like the cards spread out on the table at Mr Kinnear's, after the gentlemen had been playing the night before. [5]Hard and angular. [6]But red, a deep thick red. [7]Thick strangled tongues.

[8]It's not the ladies expected today, it's a doctor. [9]He's writing a book; the Governor's wife likes to know people who are writing books, books with forward-looking aims, it shows that she is a liberal-minded person with

advanced views, and science is making such progress, and what with modern inventions and the Crystal Palace and world knowledge assembled, who knows where we will all be in a hundred years.

[10]Where there's a doctor it's always a bad sign. [11]Even when they are not doing the killing themselves it means a death is close, and in that way they are like ravens or crows. [12]But this doctor will not hurt me, the Governor's wife promised it. [13]All he wants is to measure my head. [14]He is measuring the heads of all the criminals in the Penitentiary, to see if he can tell from the bumps on their skulls what sort of criminals they are, whether they are pickpockets or swindlers or embezzlers or criminal lunatics or murderers, she did not say Like you, Grace. [15]And then they could lock those people up before they had a chance to commit any crimes, and think how that would improve the world.

Text 41 represents two self-contained extracts from a holiday brochure aimed at couples intending to marry or honeymoon abroad in exotic locations. It's particularly suitable as a complement to the topics exemplified in Texts 22–24 inclusive (page 61), and could stimulate the collection of further similar texts for an investigative project.

TEXT 41

Jamaica

A combination of stunning tropical rainforest, spectacular waterfalls, glorious sunshine, beautiful beaches and a vibrant, colourful lifestyle is just a snapshot of what the island of Jamaica has to offer prospective newly-weds to entice them to its shores. One of the largest islands in the Caribbean, its choice of resorts ranges from laid-back Negril, with its stunning seven-mile beach, to bustling Ocho Rios and surrounding attractions. Marrying on Jamaica is both simple and affordable, with local laws permitting couples to wed just 24 hours after arrival.

Antigua

Famous for its 365 palm-fringed beaches and gentle, rolling scenery reminiscent of the English countryside, the unspoilt island of Antigua has long been a favourite place in which to get married. With its comfortable climate and tranquil air, it is also the perfect honeymoon choice. Due to its colonial history (Nelson lived here for four years), English and Caribbean influences mingle to create a particularly charming atmosphere. During your stay, take a romantic day trip to nearby Barbuda, a peaceful sanctuary with mile upon mile of pink coral beaches and exotic birdlife.

Text 42 is an extract from Mervyn Peake's *Titus Groan,* the first volume of his *Gormenghast* trilogy. In this extract we meet Titus' mother, the Countess Gertrude. This passage would be particularly useful while working through the material in Chapter 4.

TEXT 42

[1]She was seated in her bedroom. [2]Her feet were planted widely apart as though for all time. [3]Her elbows weighed on her knees, from between which the draperies of her skirt sagged in heavy U-shaped folds. [4]In her hands was a paper-covered book, with a coffee-stain across its cover and with as many dogs' ears as it had pages. [5]She was reading aloud in a deep voice that rose above the steady drone of a hundred cats. [6]They filled the room. [7]Whiter than the tallow that hung from the candelabra or lay broken on the table of birdseed. [8]Whiter than the pillows on the bed. [9]They sat everywhere. [10]The counterpane was hidden with them. [11]The table, the cupboards, the couch, all was luxuriant with harvest, white as death, but the richest crop was all about her feet where a cluster of white faces stared up into her own. [12]Every luminous, slit-pupilled eye was upon her. [13]The only movement lay in the vibration in their throats. [14]The voice of the Countess moved on like a laden ship upon a purring tide.

And finally Text 43, this time a poem, *Light Hotel* by Peter Redgrove, written in 1979. Poetry, of course, often displays marked or deviant grammatical patterns for a number of reasons. Nevertheless, an examination of the cohesive devices employed can be very revealing, though as we've remarked earlier (page 112) this approach is only one of several possible. This text should be examined only after at least some of the cohesion exercises in Chapter 6 have been attempted.

Whereas in prose the basic unit of analysis is normally the sentence, in poetry it often makes more sense to choose a smaller unit, principally because of the concentrated nature of a poem's construction and meaning. The line is frequently a more useful unit – an alternative might be the stanza where this is relatively short – and so it's therefore suggested that in drawing up your table as outlined on page 98, you substitute 'Line Number' for 'Sentence Number.' You then work through the poem systematically from line 1 to the title (which is significant in poetry), line 2 to line 1, line 3 to line 2, and so on. You should find that tabulating the links in this way provides a clearer picture of the complex and integrated nature of the patterning. You'll also appreciate that if at this level of analysis you merely highlight and draw connecting lines on the actual poem, you'll probably all but obliterate the text!

TEXT 43

Light Hotel

The little girl riding the fallen tree like a spindly horse,

Like a queen mounted on a green spider;

The little girl's white flesh is so sacred, so queenly,

I love and fear it so much

Carefully I think only of her dress,

Her foliate dress that falls in dry green pleats,

Or think as I look away from her sunlit face

How the sunlight holds a great conference in a sandgrain

With its plate-glass terraces and vista-windows of gold-tinge,

Then how the moon will hold her conference in the same sealed chamber.

In between times the non-staff have no clearing to do, no ashes to empty,

No glasses to polish, the light simply passes, great guest,

The light simply passes from the hotel, it is left untouched,

And above the million sand-grains, the one girl swishing her wide green horse.

Peter Redgrave

Index